On Natural Capital

On Natural Capital

The Value of the World Around Us

PARTHA DASGUPTA

WITNESS
BOOKS

WITNESS BOOKS

UK | USA | Canada | Ireland | Australia
India | New Zealand | South Africa

Witness Books is part of the Penguin Random House group of companies
whose addresses can be found at global.penguinrandomhouse.com

Penguin Random House UK
One Embassy Gardens, 8 Viaduct Gardens, London SW11 7BW

penguin.co.uk
global.penguinrandomhouse.com

First published by Witness Books in 2025

1

Typeset in 12.6/17.2pt Dante MT Std by Six Red Marbles UK, Thetford, Norfolk
Printed and bound in India by Manipal Technologies Limited

The authorised representative in the EEA is Penguin Random House Ireland,
Morrison Chambers, 32 Nassau Street, Dublin D02 YH68

A CIP catalogue record for this book is available from the British Library

Hardback ISBN 9781529144192
Trade Paperback ISBN 9781529144208

To Carol

Violence may be committed against God
When we deny and curse him in our hearts
Or when we scorn Nature and her bounty

Dante, *Inferno*, Canto II, lines 46–48
(trans. Robert Hollander and Jean Hollander)

Contents

Preface

This book has grown out of a report I prepared in 2021 at the invitation of the UK's Chancellor of the Exchequer to write a review of the economics of biodiversity. Behind the invitation was no doubt the feeling, widely shared among the public, that something is not right with the character of economic development the world has experienced in recent decades. It has been rapid, but it has also been accompanied by continual degradation, even desecration, of the natural environment. Climate change is one global sign of that degradation, biodiversity loss is another.

Accepting the Chancellor's invitation was easy, as I had been working for more than four decades round the idea of biodiversity, on themes across population numbers, our living standards and the environment. But I also knew what the Chancellor had asked for could not be a 'review', for there was no economics of biodiversity *to* review. One could find a substantial body of work in what is known as 'environmental and resource economics', but it hadn't been put together to create something that could be called the economics of biodiversity. Among other things, population numbers were taken as given in the studies, so possible demographic pressures on the biosphere were not discussed. But even that limited literature was ignored in growth and development economics, and in the economics of poverty. As taught and practised in academia, national treasuries and international organisations, received economics mentioned Nature only in asides. If she was to be found there, it would be as an acknowledgement of climate change – that too, as a mere add-on.

Why has environmental and resource economics ignored possibly vital factors driving economic change, such as population numbers, and why has the wider body of economic thinking ignored environmental and resource economics? Research in economics, like I imagine in other scientific disciplines, mostly involves working on problems others are also currently working on. Each publication is an incremental step on what has come before. Moreover, we economists work with models of those features of the world we want to study in detail, keeping all else in the background. Models are thus parables, even caricatures; some say they are like toys. But that is their point, for experience shows that toy models, if constructed with judgement and skill, are illuminating (by which I mean they have explanatory power and are open to empirical testing). Large numerical models as those in use by national treasuries, central banks and international organisations are, of course, necessary for making forecasts and charting options for policy; but here I am talking of models designed to offer insights into the workings of our economies and identifying the scope of policies to improve things. The harder task, and there have been successful attempts from time to time, is to put these tiny models together like pieces of embroidery in what becomes a tapestry, to give us an overarching conceptual framework that ties together a class of seemingly unconnected phenomena. Mostly, though, we economists construct and analyse those tiny models, check whether they add to our understanding and return to construct further toy models, in an iterative process, without necessarily an overarching view, which is to say, at any moment, advances in economics are hugely dependent on what has been accomplished in the recent past. A shift in the agenda of research, even when the evidence calls for it, is often near impossible to bring about. Entities, such as Nature, that have been absent in journal articles and textbooks over the years, remain absent. Economic historians call this 'path dependence'.

If the biosphere (I am using 'biosphere' as a more scientific version of Nature) had been included when models of long-run economic development and, by extension, the economics of poverty were being constructed in the 1950s and '60s, the dominant mode of economic thinking today would have been very different, and I would not be writing this preface now. There are four interconnected reasons it wasn't.

First, ecology in the way it has developed in recent decades was in its infancy, and few ecologists searched for signs of strains at a planetary scale. That they didn't is the second reason, which is that in the immediate post-war years the global economy was not large enough to have stretched the biosphere's outer limits.

The two were aided by a third reason, which is that Western economies had for a long while outsourced their 'biodiversity needs' to poor, tropical countries. If a supply source of a primary product dried up at one place, there would be another place to go to, or there would be scope to develop substitutes domestically, perhaps using a set of different primary products from another foreign source. Degradation of local ecosystems in the tropics had been alarming even then, and many rural communities in the tropics experienced biodiversity loss, but official economic thinking – even official thinking on poverty and development – saw Nature as infinite in scope and capacity.

The fourth reason is that the post-war world has enjoyed unprecedented success in raising the standard of living. Today's economic landscape would have been wholly unrecognisable in 1950. The global economy has grown more than 15-fold; per capita income has increased by a multiple of five to nearly 20,000 international dollars a year; and absolute poverty has declined from encompassing around 60 per cent of the world's population to under 10 per cent. All this despite the global population having increased from 2.5 billion to more than 8.1 billion. As economic commentators in recent years have repeatedly observed, humanity has never had it so good.

This extraordinary achievement was made possible by the accumulation of 'produced capital' (the term used to describe the physical, tangible assets such as roads, ports, buildings and machines), 'human capital' (intangible assets such as health, education, aptitude) and ideas (science and technology). The accumulation process transformed entire landscapes into agricultural fields as far as the eye can see and built gleaming metropolises across the globe. That success has influenced the framing of economic problems and the search for ways to spread the good fortune everywhere to those who have been left behind.

But our global success has come with an increasingly impoverished biosphere, caused by mining, quarrying and land-use changes, and the pollution that goes with them. One sign of that impoverishment has been the extinction of species, currently at 100 to 1,000 times the average extinction rates in the previous several million years. Another sign has been a decline in the biosphere's ability to meet our demands for its goods and services sustainably. The character of the global economy can be pictured on a coin: one side displaying skyscrapers, plantations, agricultural fields, animal farms and highways in all parts of the world; the other side depicting shrunken lakes, an increasingly erratic climate, dead oceanic zones, desiccated forests, bleached coral reefs and infertile watersheds.

If that other side is absent from received economics, it is because today's decision makers, in both private and public institutions, are yesterday's students. The mutual influence of academic economics and decision making in the world at large and the depth of their combined imprint on the public's imagination are hard to overestimate. If biodiversity is absent from official economic reckoning today – leading economics journals rarely publish articles on natural capital – it is because Nature has been absent from economics all along.

The Chancellor's invitation therefore offered me an opportunity to prepare a report that puts together the ideas found in environmental and resource economics, and expand it to the larger concern, perhaps the largest there is for social scientists: how we should read our place in the world as we go about our daily lives. Biodiversity, of which we are ourselves a part, would then appear seamlessly in the study because it is an integral part of Nature. No doubt preparing such a report was a tall order, but my Treasury team, drawn from government departments and non-government organisations, told me they expected nothing less.

As I had been working closely for some years with ecologists, I wanted to build my report on two disciplines: ecology and economics. They have in any case much to say to each other, starting with a shared prefix 'eco', whose root is the Greek *oikos*, meaning house or habitat. But 'house' or 'habitat' could refer to a household, community, district, nation, region or even the whole world. Which is why it was clear to me that the report would have a wide reach.

However, differences in the way people and their communities fashion lives tell us that they do not experience degradation of Nature in the same way. Food, drinkable water, clothing, warmth, a roof over one's head, clean air, a sense of belonging, participating with others in one's community and a reason for hope are no doubt universal needs, but the emphasis people place on the goods and services Nature supplies differs widely. To farmers in sub-Saharan Africa, the most important concern could be declining sources of water and increasing variability in rainfall in the foreground of global climate change. To indigenous populations in Amazonia it may be eviction not just from their physical home, but from their spiritual home too. To inhabitants of shanty towns everywhere, the worry may be the infections they are exposed to from open sewers. To the suburban household in the UK, it may be the absence of bees and butterflies in the garden. To residents of megacities, it could be the poisonous air they breathe. To the multinational company, it may be the worry about supply chains, as disruptions to the biosphere make old sources of primary products unreliable and investments generally more risky. To governments in some places, it may be the call by citizens, even children, to stem global climate change. And to people everywhere today, it may be the ways in which those varied experiences combine and give rise to environmental problems that affect us all, not least the COVID-19 pandemic and other emerging infectious diseases, of which land-use change and species exploitation are major drivers.

That is why the final report I submitted in February 2021 to the UK Treasury, *The Economics of Biodiversity: The Dasgupta Review* (henceforth, *Review*) was 601 pages long, and why the text was interspersed with boxes, annexes and starred chapters containing analysis conducted in the language of mathematics.*

I was therefore delighted when Witness Books, a part of Penguin Random House, asked me to prepare a book for the general reader that captures the ideas from the *Review*. As a lifelong academic, my audience has invariably been fellow academics, and so it took me a while to imagine who my reader is. But while preparing drafts of the early chapters, I gravitated to the person for whom this book is now meant:

I imagine her to be someone not so much interested in the *Review* as in wanting to know how to structure her thinking about problems that worry her. She is a concerned

---

* The *Review*, with added material, has now been published by Cambridge University Press. See Dasgupta (2024).

citizen. She wants to understand how it can be that even with the best of intentions individual choices can (and do) lead to outcomes that are worse for everyone than they could have been. She is dissatisfied with the answer she hears often; that it has all to do with 'externalities' – the unaccounted consequences for others of one's actions – because she feels that giving a label to a phenomenon should be the *conclusion* of an explanation, not its beginning.

My reader doesn't necessarily know mathematics but does not want me to avoid technicalities when needed. Being told that human activities are now so extensive as to have given rise to an ecological overreach, she asks not only why that has happened, but also how we can tell. She is dissatisfied with having to read repeatedly in the progressive media that gross domestic product (GDP) is an inadequate measure of economic performance; she wants to know what should replace it and why. Nor does she want to be told that any such index will be hard to estimate, whereas GDP figures can be relied upon; for she believes estimates that are vaguely right are a lot better than those that are precisely wrong. My reader is eager for all this because she is convinced that without an appreciation of the place of the human economy in Nature, which is another way saying *our* place in Nature, environmental concerns will remain reserved for Sundays, and that on weekdays we will continue to be guided by an economics that is bereft of Nature. My reader is someone willing to work hard with me.

My understanding of our place in Nature has grown in the years since the *Review* was submitted to the UK Treasury in 2021. So, it took me a while to decide how to write a book that conveys the overarching ideas in the *Review* but builds entirely on the central empirical finding of recent years on the character of the global economy, which is that the demands we today make for Nature's goods and services far exceed her ability to supply them on a sustainable basis. The difference between the two is a measure of the human ecological overreach.

The first half of the book draws on ecology to explain what the overreach means, and it concludes with the single formula I have been obliged to introduce, as it identifies the determinants of the two sides of the gap between 'demand' and 'sustainable supply'. The latter half of the book uses economics to uncover the factors that explain how those determinants relate to one another over time and what options humanity has for closing the gap.

There are several ways in which this book could have been structured. The one I have followed tries all the while to convey the subject's beauty and intellectual dazzle. Moreover, I have steered away from styles of exposition where the current understanding of a subject is presented as a seamless, completed whole. I have frequently paused to offer alternative explanations of a phenomenon and shown that they should be rejected either because they are shallow or, worse, because they are wrong.

I have deliberately framed the body of the book to read Nature in anthropocentric terms, that is, in terms of her value to us, that is, to humans. This includes not just the instrumental value to us of her goods and services, but also the intrinsic value we see in her. Nevertheless, the viewpoint misses something of supreme importance; for there can be a temptation to read intrinsic value as the worth we only attribute to places of beauty, and that is self-indulgence. So, in the final chapter I discuss whether Nature has a worth that is *external* to us. The book concludes with a discussion of what loss we suffer when our actions increase the risk of human extinction.

The absence of Nature from mainstream economic thinking points to a paradox. Economic commentators rightly demand that public policies should be evidence-based and know that the evidence that is collected would be of no use if it were built on a misleading conception of the human condition; for faulty models produce spurious evidence. But they should also know that systems of thought that do not acknowledge humanity's embeddedness in Nature when used to project present and future possibilities can be misleading. The findings of ecologists and Earth scientists have demonstrated that such systems of thought can mislead so hugely that policies based on them not only endanger future generations, but also damage the lives of the world's contemporary poor. The enormously large and influential literature on growth and development economics and the economics of poverty remains impoverished on this count. It reads as an elaborate exercise in collective solipsism. This book is an attempt to redress this.

Partha Dasgupta, St John's College, Cambridge

CHAPTER I

Nature Is an Asset

In tropical and sub-tropical regions, there are shallow coastal estuaries and neighbouring mudflats inhabited by salt-tolerant evergreen trees and shrubs, known collectively as mangroves. Propping themselves above the water level with stilt-like structures called prop roots, mangroves adjacent to the coastline accommodate the daily rise and fall of tides. The barks of prop roots store salt, and as the muddy soil is low in oxygen, they have evolved also to absorb oxygen directly from the air. On mudflats a bit further inland, mangroves develop root-like structures that stick up out of the soil for breathing. Mangrove leaves photosynthesise, conserve water and regulate toxic salts.

Like storm walls, mangroves are barriers against cyclones and storms, and a buffer against floods. They prevent saltwater from entering inland during storm surges and help to regenerate life in coastal waters by exporting nutrients and waste products. The silence you experience as you paddle your boat in a mangrove swamp, while avoiding the tangled, gnarled trees of the forest, is like visiting a primeval world of darkness interspersed by the occasional sunbeam entering through small openings in a dense canopy. That

A mangrove forest in the Sundarbans, near the Bay of Bengal (Getty Images)

silence is not stillness, though, for it cloaks the habits and activities of numerous species of fish, birds, insects, worms, molluscs, amphibians, crustaceans, reptiles, even big cats, that make the place their home. Bacteria and fungi contribute to the forest's rhythms by decomposing its residues and the material that enters it from inland.

The eerie feeling of being able to sense Nature's workings in the raw puts to rest the idea that serene beauty resides only in tidiness. We have grown to see beauty in an ordered Nature, neat and organised, as in the artist's landscape. But rotting leaves and decaying barks floating in the muddy waters of a mangrove forest make us aware of the rhythms of Nature. What we previously saw as ugly in her underbelly now appears both serene and beautiful.

There are more than 80 species of mangroves, spread

over some 100 countries. Mangrove forests cover only a thousandth of Earth's land surface, but they store in their branches, roots and sediment up to ten times the quantity of carbon per hectare in temperate forests. Only marshlands and seagrasses have comparable ability to sequester carbon.

People live in and around mangrove forest areas, shaping and reshaping them. More than 7 million people inhabit the Sundarbans (literally, 'beautiful forests'), which are a cluster of islands in the Bay of Bengal. The world's largest mangrove area, the Sundarbans (in Bengali, the name of the entity is in the singular, and pronounced as in 'Shundorbon') lie at the confluence of the Ganges, Brahmaputra and Meghna rivers as they flow into the bay. Partly in Bangladesh, partly in India, a portion of the region is a UNESCO World Heritage Site. Today the area is made up of mangrove forests, waterways and forest clearings. People survive there by using mangrove wood as building material, collecting honey and pharmaceuticals, and harvesting fibres to thatch homes. They make a living by fishing, cultivating rice in paddy fields as subsistence farmers, working in aquaculture at the edges of the area, selling artefacts from material collected from the forest (wood, barks, shells, stones), and serving as boatmen in a growing tourist industry. Spirits – Bonbibi (the mistress of the forest) and Ghazibaba (Warrior) – guard the forest and protect inhabitants against storms and cyclones. It is said Bonbibi protects them against snakes and crocodiles as well.

In their beauty and functionality, their natural rhythms and economic value, mangrove forests are microcosms of the biosphere, the part of Earth that is occupied by living organisms. Studying them, like studying other living systems, offers us a glimpse of Nature's workings. We need to have a glimpse of those workings here, for otherwise we would not appreciate why Nature is a capital asset, indeed, why she is our most precious asset. As we are embedded in Nature, we would then also come to appreciate that she is both a means and ends in our lives.

Nature's Rhythms

Movement is a pervasive feature of Nature: the wind blows, rivers flow, birds and insects fly, animals travel, fish swim, the oceans circulate, and even snails leave a trail. Without that movement, we would not exist, let alone thrive as we have. Less visible are the changes that take place when plants die and are converted into soil by the actions of organisms – bacteria and fungi – that also live and die.

Living systems make use of non-living material and transform them. Water, carbon and nitrogen cycles, familiar from our school geography classes, are expressions of that. One manifestation of this is when winds blow parallel to coastlines, pushing surface water offshore. Water, rich in nitrogen and phosphorus compounds, then rises from the ocean deep and fertilises surface water, encouraging the growth of microscopic algae, which are food for fish, marine mammals and seabirds.

Nature's rhythms such as the seasons influence the regeneration patterns of the living world. The annual regeneration of deciduous forests is an example, as are seasonal changes in wildflower meadows. The daily tides shape the character of marshes, coastal fisheries, bird populations and their regeneration patterns. Regeneration can also appear as successions, where the mix of species and their habitat in an area change over time owing to a shock or disturbance, such as a volcanic eruption, a bush fire, a flood or the outbreak of a disease. Such disturbances are almost always unexpected. But what we regard to have been a shock could have been a tipping-point phenomenon of a changing factor influencing the living system, as in the sudden growth of algae in a freshwater lake brought about by phosphorus run-off from neighbouring farms. On the other hand, the cause could itself be cyclical, such as a succession of ice ages, which lead forests to alternate inhabiting and then receding from temperate regions. The time frame matters. A population could also display a regular beat, perhaps lying dormant over long stretches of time, even if over short intervals it behaves chaotically. The occasional, unpredictable outburst of locusts is a well-known example. But the population in time crashes as it faces barriers to further expansion.

Nature's beats differ vastly in their length. Bacteria can survive for an hour or more on surfaces, frogs live for ten to twelve years, mangrove trees for a hundred years, oak trees for as long as a thousand years, mushrooms live from between one and two days up to many years, and there are networks of fungi species that live up to a hundred or thousand years. The rhythms of even weakly connected oscillating objects can synchronise, such as linked pendula, singing crickets, and so on. Moreover, birth and death cycles can get locked in a population to form unique patterns.

There are species of cicada that emerge synchronically every 17 years but live as adults for only 3–4 weeks.

Physical processes have their beat and rhythm too. Microclimates follow daily weather patterns; the global climate follows an annual cycle; water in the deep oceans takes 500 years to make a complete journey round Earth; the contribution of the planet's eccentricities as it rotates on its axis and revolves round the Sun together set a figure of 100,000 years or more for ice ages; and so on. And there are models devised by Earth scientists that project the formation and breakup of super continents over the course of 200–400 million years. Most of the factors affecting Nature's constituent parts are unknown. We are thus drawn into identifying what seem to us to be dominant ones and then discerning cycles.

Regeneration of its living parts is how the biosphere regulates itself. Mostly, though, the processes driving regeneration are invisible to the naked eye and silent to the human ear. We do not see or hear the activities of fungal masses as they reconstruct soil and enable plants to live, without which life as we know it would not exist. And we can neither see nor hear the processes in the oceans that are constantly decomposing dead organisms and burying the carbon in their bed.

Ecosystems

The biosphere is spatially so varied that it is necessary to study its parts separately, then their connections, then back to the parts to gain a more informed picture of them – and so on, in a never-ending search for deeper understanding. A schema that has proved to be fruitful is to think of the biosphere as a tapestry of ecological systems, or 'ecosystems'; a complex of living organisms (plants, animals, fungi and microorganisms) and their non-living environment in a particular location that together combine to control such natural processes as energy flow and material recycling. They are shaped by the multitude of Nature's beats and rhythms and in turn shape them.

The looseness in the definition of ecosystems is deliberate: what we regard to be an ecosystem depends on the point of our enquiry. Mangrove forests are ecosystems, as are watersheds, wetlands, marshes, deserts and coral reefs. Agricultural land, plantations, animal farms, freshwater lakes, rainforests, coastal fisheries, estuaries, the atmosphere and the oceans are also ecosystems. But so are the individual life forms in them. The garden pond is an ecosystem, as are the plants and amphibians that thrive in it. Thus, ecosystems can be 'nested', in that they can be whole while simultaneously being part of something larger.

Nor are ecosystems tightly knit entities; they often overlap and can blend into one another. The Okavango River comes down from the hills of Angola and waters grasslands in northern Zimbabwe. As the river loses its energy, grass gives way to shrubs. And then, as the Okavango sinks into the ground, shrubs give way to the pebbly desert of the Kalahari. But there are ecosystems that have strong interactions among their own constituents and weak interactions across their boundaries, as in the visible breaks between the oases and deserts of Egypt. The boundaries accentuate differences in material composition, distribution of organisms, soil types, depth of a body of water, and so on.

Ecosystems differ in their spatial reach (the Amazon rainforest is an ecosystem, as is the collection of micro-organisms occupying the gut of an animal, or even a droplet of water) and in their rhythmic time (hours for bacterial colonies, decades for boreal forests). Some ecosystems cover regions (the Mekong River basin), some are volcanic islands (Micronesia), others involve clusters of towns (micro-watersheds in the Ethiopian highlands) or are confined to a village (ponds in Bangladesh).

That Nature's rhythms are embedded in the functioning of ecosystems is vividly illustrated in lake fisheries. The canonical or archetypal version of a lake fishery imagines a deterministic world in which the lake ecosystem supplies a constant flow of nutrients and living material, which supports a dominant fish population. Over their lifetime adult fish produce eggs and in due course die. Meanwhile, those eggs that survived and became adults produce eggs and in due course also die, and the cycle goes on.

In the absence of predators, the fishery's regeneration rate in any period – fisheries economists call it the 'yield' – is the difference between the number of births and the number of deaths. Should the rate in any period be positive, the stock in the next period would be bigger than the current stock; if it were negative, the stock in the next period would be smaller. It is a feature of the ecosystem that if the stock were below a critical size – ecologists call it a 'threshold' (the point L in Fig. 1.1) – the population would not be viable. The number of deaths would be greater than the number of births, which means that in due course the population would die, perhaps to be replaced by a different species of fish, small in numbers initially and waiting in the wings to seize its chance, so to speak. But if the stock was to exceed the threshold, ever so slightly, the dynamics of the fish population would be entirely different.* With a positive yield, the stock would increase in size period by period, but it would increase at a diminishing rate because the larger the stock, the smaller the food supply per fish. At large sizes the constancy of the food supply would bite so heavily that the yield would decline with further increases in stock, until becoming negative at very large population sizes (beyond the point *K* in Fig. 1.1). Thus, if left alone, the fishery would settle at the size, *K*, where the yield is zero. Ecologists say that the yield is zero at that population size because the

FIG.1.1 RELATIONSHIP BETWEEN STOCK OF FISH AND ITS YIELD

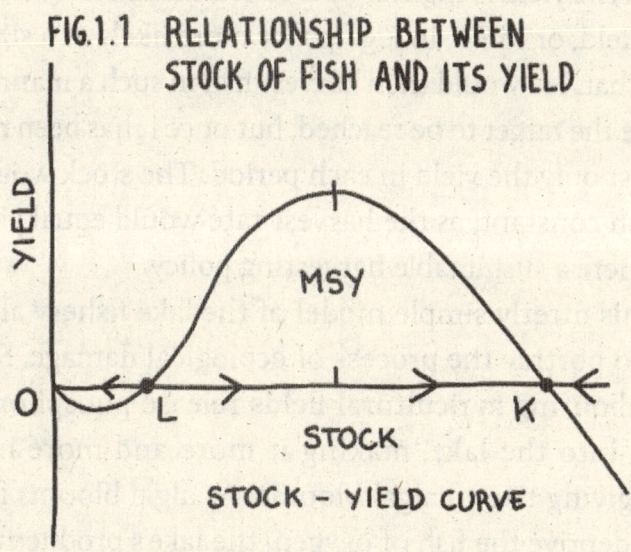

STOCK – YIELD CURVE

* Thus *L* is a tipping point.

fishery has reached the lake's 'carrying capacity'. (In Fig. 1.1 K is the carrying capacity.) But that does not mean the lake ecosystem has ceased renewing itself at carrying capacity. Yield is zero because births equal deaths, not because there are no births. Fig. 1.1 depicts the relationship between the stock of fish and its yield.

Notice that there is ample scope for fishermen to harvest fish in the lake, for yield is positive for a range of stock sizes. But because of the fishermen's activities, there is a difference between the fishery's yield and its regeneration rate. The difference between the two is the rate at which fish is harvested. An astute fisherman, assuming he has no competitor and assuming it is profitable for him to harvest fish from the lake, would target a stock size in that range, say, the size at which the yield is highest (it is called the maximum sustainable yield, or MSY, in Fig. 1.1), or more likely at a size lower than that. He would then harvest fish in such a manner as to enable the target to be reached, but once it has been reached, harvest only the yield in each period. The stock would then remain constant, as the harvest rate would equal yield. We have here a sustainable harvesting policy.

This utterly simple model of the lake fishery allows us also to portray the process of ecological damage. Suppose neighbouring agricultural fields release phosphorus that seeps into the lake, making it more and more nutrient rich, giving rise to algal blooms. As algal blooms increasingly deprive the fish of oxygen, the lake's productivity as a fishery declines, which means the stock–yield curve in Fig. 1.1 moves downward and leftward and disappears entirely when the blooms overwhelm the lake ecosystem, turning it into a dead lake.

An alternative setting in which the fishery would be destroyed is where there are many fishermen, all of whom enjoy sufficiently low harvesting costs to make fishing worthwhile. Consider the case where no one has property rights over the lake, that is, anyone can catch as much fish as they like. The fishery in this case is what is known as an 'open access resource'. Under an open access regime, with low harvesting costs, total catch in each period would exceed the maximum sustainable yield, and the fish stock over time would be exhausted. Ocean fisheries are not yet depleted, but in large areas they are under threat of exhaustion, as in the case of the North Sea cod population. To prevent exhaustion, communities impose fishing regulations. In some places regulations are enforced by entry charges, taxes on the catch, or even quantity regulations on how much a fisherman is permitted to catch.

The model of the freshwater lake says that even though individual organisms in an ecosystem are born, survive for a period and then die, the ecosystem continues to exist so long as it is not overexploited or damaged by pollution. This has a wider, deeper moral. Each of us is an entity in many ecosystems, and we each harbour within us microbial ecosystems. Nature is the largest ecosystem of which we are an element. She is our home. Being embedded in her, we are entirely dependent on her, not just for survival but for our wellbeing too. We are dependent entirely on Nature because she continually produces goods and services that we need and enjoy.

Goods and Services

In common parlance the terms 'goods' and 'services' are distinguished by how durable they are. Services appear fleetingly, goods last for a while. A car is a 'good'. If maintained with care, it may give its owner journeys amounting to 200,000 miles. In contrast, a mile's journey is a service. The value of an automobile to its owner is the value attributable by her to the miles it is anticipated to deliver over its lifetime less its operating costs. To be sure, cars, like any other good, depreciate over time, which is why on occasion they need repair and the replacement of parts. So, the operating costs include the costs of repair and maintenance. But the costs should also include the damage suffered by others from the carbon the car emits and the microscopic particles its rubber tyres spew when providing its service.

Such environmental costs are typically not included in the car's market price, nor in its running costs. They do not appear in the measures we rely on to assess economic performance, such as GDP. As we will see, the losses arising from those costs are so huge today that they contribute to making contemporary economic development policies unsustainable.

We refer to goods as 'assets' if they have a positive value to us. Economists call them 'capital assets', sometimes also 'capital goods'. The qualifier in the first case is redundant, in the latter it simply replaces the term durable. But it has proved so tempting to call assets capital goods that the term now stretches to include knowledge (as in 'knowledge capital'); the law, government, the market system and financial institutions (as in 'institutional capital'); mutual trust, social norms and group solidarity (as in 'social capital'); culture and personal norms, and the rituals that go with them (as in 'cultural capital'); and even religion (as in 'religious capital').

Economists were until relatively recently more reticent and confined the use of the term capital assets to assets that are measurable, most notably to those that are tangible, alienable (which means that ownership can be transferred) and excludable (the owner can exclude others from its use), such as a writing desk. Their reasoning had been that because tangible, alienable and excludable assets are marketable, their value to people can be inferred from their market prices. Today, though, economists also include on their list tangible, inalienable, non-excludable assets (the oceans); intangible, alienable, excludable assets (the view from one's home); even intangible, inalienable assets (personal health, publicly available knowledge). Because such assets are mostly not traded in markets, economists have had to devise ingenious methods to determine the value that should be placed on them.

Humanity's material advancement across millennia has been made possible by our invention of newer and newer varieties of what, for early humans, we reserve the term 'tools'. Today we call tools 'produced capital'. Roads, buildings, ports, ships, automobiles, furniture, machines and books are familiar examples. We have been able to discover novel ways of doing things because we have simultaneously accumulated what economists call 'human capital'. This somewhat bloodless term covers the deepest and most personal aspects of our lives, including health, education, knowledge, skills and character. But even in common parlance we use the economist's term when we say that our children are our greatest assets.

Some assets are private to oneself, such as skills, although they can be transmitted via instruction. But teaching someone skills does not deprive the teacher ownership of her own skills. So, skills are intangible, inalienable assets. Then there are 'public goods', which are assets that are non-excludable and non-rivalrous (use by a person or a group of persons does not diminish the asset's availability to others). Such assets offer a flow of services that are non-excludable and non-rivalrous. The climate is an example. A field of study such as calculus is another; it is available to us all, even if not everyone has the skills to make use of it. It is an intangible public good. Acquiring the skill to use calculus is to acquire human capital. Like produced capital, human capital depreciates, indeed we take our human capital with us when we die. In contrast, ideas (which are public goods) can in principle last forever. A piece of knowledge, for example, the formula for a manufacturing process, is a public good that can last forever. However, while in principle non-excludable, it can be converted into an excludable asset, at least for a while, by the award of a patent, meaning that only the patent holder can make use of it. Another way to make it excludable, at least for a while, is to keep it secret. However, the secret is often unlocked by rival entrepreneurs deploying reverse engineering.

The world's stock of natural resources is called by the generic name 'natural capital'. The category includes not only living organisms, but also materials and non-living organisms, such as sand, gravel and detritus. Because they all are to be found in ecosystems, we can identify items of natural capital with ecosystems and their constituents. As with produced capital, ecosystems depreciate when they are misused or are overused. But they differ from produced capital in certain ways.

1. Damage to an ecosystem is in many cases irreversible; at best the system takes a long while to recover.

2. It is not possible to replicate a depleted or degraded ecosystem. Even if restoration activities enable an ecosystem to recover, it will not be quite the same as previously. The composition of plants, animals and fungi will inevitably be different.

3. Ecosystems can collapse abruptly, without much warning. We reserve the term 'tipping' for such collapses. (The threshold population size in the lake fishery in Fig. 1.1 is a tipping point.)*

An item of natural capital can be a luxury for some even while it is a necessity for others. Many goods and services

---

* The third characteristic can also apply to produced capital, as when machines break down without notice. But produced capital does not usually possess the first characteristic, for repairs are completed rapidly in factories. Nor does it possess the second characteristic, for machines can be replicated. As always, there are exceptions to any rule: works of art, which are also examples of produced capital, are unique. It is interesting that people share all three characteristics with ecosystems, but that only reminds us that ecosystems are themselves living systems.

that are provided by watersheds are necessities for local inhabitants (forest dwellers, downstream farmers, fishermen), some are sources of revenue for commercial firms (timber companies), while others are luxuries for outsiders (eco-tourists). Some benefits accrue to those within a specific area (agricultural crops), while others spill across national boundaries (carbon sequestration).

Ecosystems supply joint products. Wetlands protect biodiversity, control floods, and supply reeds and medicinal plants, but they also produce goods that compete against one another for our attention (commercial timber, agricultural land, biodiversity). Competition among rival goods has been a prime force behind the way the biosphere has been transformed. Sadly, commercial demand frequently trumps local needs, especially under non-democratic regimes. Indigenous communities, dispersed as they often are and unconnected to modern economies, are invariably defeated in political battles over resources; their plight is rarely ever in the news.

A Three-way Classification of Assets

To invest in an asset, be it tangible (an ecosystem) or intangible (a person's or organisation's reputation) is to increase its stock. For an ecosystem the stock could be measured in quantity (e.g., biomass in the case of a forest) or quality (e.g., diversity of species) or both. In the case of a person or organisation, the stock would be the degree to which they are popular or respected. For many people, the term investment could remind them of the activities of stock-brokers, who advise clients on changes to their portfolio of financial stocks. But here we are concerned with investment in real assets, such as items of produced capital, human capital and natural capital.

The image that comes to mind when we think of investment in produced capital is of men and women in hard hats at work with bulldozers and electric drills, breaking ground or raising a tower block. Investment in human capital reminds us of reading books and attending classes. In contrast, investment in an ecosystem may mostly involve waiting for Nature to restore herself. The cost of conservation or restoration is the best alternative use to which the ecosystem could have been put. We have consistently undervalued the return on investment in natural capital and overvalued the return on produced capital, leading to the degradation of the former and the accumulation of the latter. In the process, we have vastly reduced the diversity of Nature, thereby reducing her ability to flourish.

That we use the term goods for durable objects tells us that we are limiting the use of the term to objects we view approvingly. But not all forms of natural capital have a positive value to us. Viruses that are damaging, even lethal, have a negative value. Antibiotics have been the post-war miracle for combating bacteria that kill us and other animals, but they mutate selectively in an arms race against new forms of anti-microbial drugs. And there is industrial pollution that affects the health of ecosystems and erodes non-living materials.

When we dump sewage into a stream, we damage

aquatic life by using the stream as a sink for the pollutant. The stream is the 'good', while sewage is the 'bad', and the latter is a bad because it reduces the quality of a good. Similarly with carbon emissions from our activities: the atmosphere, a good, is the sink into which the carbon is deposited. Further emissions reduce the biosphere's ability to regulate the global climate in a manner that has proved beneficial to us over the past 12,000 years or more. Emissions amount to pollution, and the global climate change that has been unleashed in consequence is damaging our daily lives.

Organisms are themselves ecosystems. Those that photosynthesise capture energy from the Sun and deploy water and carbon dioxide to produce oxygen and glucose, which is a form of sugar. The latter is broken down by the organisms to obtain energy. Plants, algae and many bacteria photosynthesise. Herbivores obtain their energy by eating plants, and carnivores by eating herbivores. Being bottom of the food chain, photosynthesising organisms are called 'primary producers'.

We have discussed ecosystems and the goods and services they produce with only examples in mind, but can we also classify them to cover the entire biosphere? In what follows I deploy the Common International Classification of Ecosystem Services (CICES), which has been built on the pioneering work of the Millennium Ecosystem Assessment (MEA, 2005), to offer a three-way classification of ecosystem goods and services, each of which we found mangrove forests to be supplying.

1. *Provisioning Goods* are those we harvest or extract from ecosystems. Their regeneration is a flow (as in, so many additional tons of mass of organic material – biomass – per year), whereas the good itself is a stock (as in, so many tons of biomass: period). Provisioning goods include food, freshwater, timber, fuel (dung, wood, twigs and leaves), fibre (grasses, cotton, wool, silk), soil, sand and gravel as building material, biochemicals and pharmaceuticals (medicines, food additives), genetic resources (genes and genetic information used for plant breeding and biotechnology) and ornamental resources (skins, shells, stones, flowers).

2. *Maintenance and Regulating Services* maintain and regulate ecosystem processes, including maintaining the gaseous composition of the atmosphere, regulating local and global climate (temperature, precipitation, winds and currents), controlling erosion (retaining soil and preventing landslides), regulating the flow of water (the timing and magnitude of runoff, flooding and aquifer recharge), purifying water and decomposing waste, regulating diseases (controlling the abundance of pathogens such as cholera and disease vectors such as mosquitoes), controlling crop/livestock pests and diseases, pollinating plants, offering protection against storms (forests and woodlands on land, mangroves and coral reefs on coasts), recycling nutrients, and maintaining the ability of primary producers to photosynthesise.

3. *Cultural Services* offer non-material benefits, including spiritual experiences and an identification with religious values.* The diversity of life has in part shaped the diversity of cultures. Moreover, various systems of thought attach spiritual and religious significance to flora and fauna. People also find aesthetic value in Nature, which finds expression in private gardens, public parks and protected areas. Ecosystems influence social relationships – social capital in coastal fishing villages takes a different form from social capital in nomadic herding and agricultural societies – and local ecosystems offer people a sense of place, a cultural landscape.

Although cultural services are supremely important for humankind, the first two types are more fundamental, for they are independent of the human presence. Provisioning goods and maintenance and regulating services evolved and formed the character of the biosphere even before humanity existed. That is why we study them for now.

Provisioning goods are Nature's 'produce' – their regeneration over a period is Nature's 'yield'. With human ingenuity provisioning goods are transformed into the final products that, when aggregated using market prices, read as gross domestic product, or GDP.

In contrast, maintenance and regulating services act upon stocks of natural capital and replenish them. By replenishment,

---

* It is perhaps more appropriate to trace these experiences and values to Nature, rather than ecosystems, because the latter is a term of recent origin.

or regeneration, we mean *net* regeneration: births minus deaths. As we noted when describing lake fisheries, there is renewal even when births equal deaths, meaning net regeneration is zero. Fungi are involved in decomposing dead material and our waste products, enabling ecosystems to regenerate; birds and insects pollinate, helping to create new life; and so on. These processes involve energy flows and material transfers, which contribute to the production of maintenance and regulating services. There is mutual feedback between provisioning goods and maintenance and regulating services.*

There is a further distinction between them. Provisioning goods are specific to ecosystems. In contrast, maintenance and regulating services are in part specific to ecosystems but in part are also global. The fish we catch is specific to the lake from which we catch the fish, and the decomposition of fallen leaves takes place largely on site by bacteria and fungi, but climate regulation involves movements of energy and materials across the globe. The difference between *drawing upon* Nature for provisioning goods and *depending on* Nature for maintenance and regulating services is all-important here. As the processes that furnish us with Nature's maintenance and regulating services are for the most part silent and invisible, their significance continues to be underestimated by us as we go about our daily lives.

---

* In the lake fishery of Fig. 1.1, fish stock is the provisioning good, whereas the yield curve is an expression of the ecosystem's maintenance and regulating services. Feedback between the stock and the ecosystem's maintenance and regulating services tells us that the stock is a factor in the parameters of the yield curve.

Substitutes and Complements

This points to a conflict between our demand for provisioning goods and our need for maintenance and regulating services. When we engage in mining, quarrying and more broadly in land-use changes accompanying expansions of crop agriculture, animal farming and plantations, which is an investment in provisioning goods, we increase food output. When we construct roads, ports and buildings, we increase the stock of produced capital, one that makes greater demand on provisioning goods (water, timber and, more broadly, biodiversity). In each such case the landscape is so transformed that the supply of Nature's maintenance and regulating services is affected, often adversely. About a third of the world's remaining wetlands were lost between 1970 and 2015. More than a third of Earth's land surface is currently used as cropland and pastures. Most new cropland has replaced forests, and most new pastureland has replaced grasslands, savannahs and shrublands.

Transformation of the landscape, taken together with the technologies we have deployed on croplands and pastures to raise their output of provisioning goods, has massively altered the composition of Nature's goods and services. We have created swathes of dead zones in coastal waters and weakened the biosphere's ability to regulate climate, among many other disasters. Biodiversity has been lost, reducing the biosphere's ability to supply maintenance and regulating services. Weakening that ability feeds back to reduce the biosphere's propensity to supply provisioning goods. We counter the reduction by deploying more produced capital (increased use of industrial fertilisers and pesticides, for example). That, however, feeds back to further weaken Nature's ability to supply maintenance and regulating services, creating a vicious cycle. As the biosphere's goods and services are the underpinnings of human societies, increases in the material standard of living will come to naught if those underpinnings are broken irreparably.

Nature's maintenance and regulating services are also *complementary* to one another: sufficiently disrupting one also disrupts the others. The complementarities arise because, as we noted previously, ecosystems supply multiple maintenance and regulating services, which is to say, they supply joint products. Tropical rainforests, rich in biodiversity, influence wind patterns, transport nutrients, decompose organic waste, recycle carbon, capture nitrogen, recycle and filter water, nurture pollinators, and so on. A desiccated forest is unable to offer any of these with vigour. Under extreme stress it flips into a shrubland. Biodiversity loss and global climate change, for another example, are deeply connected. There are bounds on the extent to which human ingenuity can be exercised to transform natural capital into produced capital and human capital without rupturing the biosphere's workings.

The ecologists Tom Lovejoy, William Laurance and their collaborators have observed that the Amazon rainforest generates half of its rainfall by recycling moisture five to six times as air masses move from the Atlantic across the basin to the west. They have estimated that at 20–30 per cent further deforestation, large swathes of the Amazon would

33

Aerial view of a depleted forest reserve in Mato Grosso State, Brazil (Alamy)

experience diminished rainfall and lengthened dry seasons, tipping the rainforest into savannah vegetation. That shift would then affect wind patterns, altering farming conditions as far away as the central US.

There are further problems. Disturbances at one location are quickly transmitted elsewhere. Crop failure in one part of the world causes food prices to rise in another in short order. The world is more connected now than previously; ecologists say it is less modular, in that it is composed of fewer distinct subsystems. That has made Nature less resilient. Interregional movement of people and goods rapidly conveys diseases and invasive species across the globe. Moreover, increased human activity has eaten into the diversity of life forms. That in turn has reduced the diversity of ecosystems and thereby, as we will see in Chapter 2, their productivity.

At its most extreme, the situation can be seen as a house of cards. Remove one card and the house collapses. Fortunately, the biosphere is not a house of cards. Nature continues to show resilience, but we humans are now so ingenious that we would be able to reduce her to a fragile house of cards if we put our mind to it.

CHAPTER 2

How Biodiversity Works

Biological diversity, or biodiversity for short, means the diversity of life. Human-induced reductions in biodiversity are not an ethically neutral phenomenon, for life forms are lost. But biodiversity also has instrumental value to us and to other life forms because it contributes to the productivity of ecosystems. Nature's ability to supply maintenance and regulating services is weakened when biodiversity declines, and that reduces her ability to supply provisioning goods, which we rely on to make the goods we consume. So, provisioning goods are our direct demands from Nature. In contrast, our dependence on maintenance and regulating services is indirect – we don't 'consume' them – but they are essential for the supply of provisioning goods.

Unfortunately, it is all too easy for us to ignore the chain connecting the methods we adopt to harvest and extract provisioning goods and their effect on Nature's ability to supply maintenance and regulating services. For example, deploying modern chemicals in agriculture or transforming the landscape to create more land to produce yet more provisioning goods reduces biodiversity; and that imposes yet more pressure on Nature's ability to supply maintenance and regulating services, which in turn affects Nature's ability to supply provisioning goods. There is mutual feedback here. That is why it is important to understand the significance of biodiversity from an economic perspective if we ever wish to achieve sustainable consumption.

Although biodiversity means the diversity of life in all its forms, it is commonly taken to mean the number of species of organisms that inhabit Earth. By a species we mean a population whose members can interbreed freely under natural conditions. As in the case of ecosystems, the definition is not airtight ('natural conditions' are hard to pin down), but as we confirm below, it is invaluable.

Species is the lowest rung in the hierarchical classification of life forms, which runs as species, genus, family, order, class, phylum and kingdom. Each rung higher than that of species is a cluster of species that resemble one another and are thought to share a common ancestry. Mathematicians would say that the division (or partition) of all living forms in terms of species is finer than the division of all living forms in terms of genera (the plural of genus), which in turn is finer than the division in terms of families, and so on. To illustrate, a pair of organisms that are not of the same species (say, alder flycatchers, which are residents of alder swamps and wet thickets, and yellow-bellied flycatchers, which are residents of coniferous woods and cold bogs) can be members of the same genus (*Empidonax*), but a pair of organisms that are not of the same genus cannot belong to the same species; organisms that are not of the same genus – say, tigers (they are of genus *Panthera*) and domestic cats (they are of genus *Felis*) – can be members of the same family (Felidae), but a pair of organisms that are not of the same family cannot belong to the same genus; and so forth.

Being the lowest rung in the classification (or the finest division, the two come to the same thing), the concept of species is central to the study of biodiversity. The ecologist Edward O. Wilson called it 'the holy grail of systematic biology'.

An organism's habitat is a place in an ecosystem where it can find and gather food, select a mate and reproduce successfully. The familiar robin's habitat, for instance, is typically a few adjacent suburban gardens, which it guards fiercely. At the other end of the spectrum are blue whales, which undertake a 4,000-mile migration seasonally between summer feeding grounds and winter breeding grounds. The evolution of life takes place in a process that sees a continual extinction of species together with the emergence of new species. New species emerge when a population splits into two or more sub-populations due to storms, chance appearance of barriers, and even small differences in food sources or the availability of sunlight in neighbouring forest patches. Each sub-population then lives in its own habitat. Genetic mutations over time make the separated sub-populations so different that members of one are unable to breed with those of another. The process is called speciation.

Biologists studying the evolution of life have found it useful to classify life forms in other ways and locate the time of their emergence from Earth's bio-geochemical signatures, such as fossilised deposits of flora and fauna, phosphorus and nitrogen compounds, gravel, sand and rocks. By sequencing the genetic material in cells fossilised in ancient rocks, palaeo-biologists estimate that bacteria and archaea (which, like bacteria, are a type of single-cell organism) emerged on Earth some 3.5 billion years ago; organisms that can photosynthesise (primary producers), including many evolved forms of bacteria, appeared nearly 3 billion years ago; and organisms with cells containing a distinct nucleus that houses genetic material in the form of chromosomes – such organisms are called 'eukaryotes' – some 1.8 billion years ago. Oxygen levels began to rise approximately 650 million years ago, possibly even earlier; plants, animals and fungi emerged on land 480 million years ago, maybe more; forests appeared around 370 million years ago; and modern groups such as mammals, birds, reptiles and land plants originated about 200 million years ago. That background helps us to appreciate that our own species, *Homo sapiens*, is of very recent origin, having emerged only about 200,000 years ago, in Africa.

Fossil records suggest that on average, eukaryote species from emergence to extinction last for 5 to 10 million years, and mammal species for only 1 million years. More than 99 per cent of the approximately 5 billion (eukaryote) species that are thought to have existed are now extinct.

How do scientists arrive at these estimates? Extinction rates of various taxonomic groups, when their presence does not appear in fossil records, are deduced from such bio-geochemical signatures as oxygen in ice cores. Radiometric methods are deployed for dating ancient events. Carbon dating can be used effectively for fossils up to 60,000 years old or more. For older fossils, the clock frequently used is potassium-40, whose quantities halve every 1.25 million years. For even older fossils, longer lasting radioactive elements such as ribudium-87, with a half-life of 48.8 billion years, are needed.

These and other related methods enable geo-scientists to study Earth's past. There have been five global mass extinction events, when at least 75 per cent of eukaryote species became extinct in the relatively short period of some 2 million years on each occasion. The one common reason behind the mass extinctions was a sequence of natural events that altered the character of the biosphere so much as to make life for most existing species impossible. The first mass extinction occurred about 540 million years ago, the fifth some 66 million years ago.

Following each extinction event, biodiversity increased. Paleo-biologists posit that the emergence of new species in a depleted Earth altered the environment in ways that made the biosphere gradually more habitable, meaning that there was positive feedback between the emergence of new species and physical conditions favourable to supporting life. There was, for example, a rise in the concentration of oxygen in a relatively depleted atmosphere following the emergence of new forms of photosynthesising organisms.

Nature's Diversity

Some 15,000–18,000 species of eukaryotes are identified each year. They are identified from collections in such storehouses as natural history museums and botanical gardens, fed by collectors in forests, islands, seashores, even cities. (One much publicised method of collecting samples involves shaking habitats in canopies of tropical rainforests and examining the species that rain down.) Taxonomists compare species richness in different collections of insects from temperate and tropical regions, and extrapolate the ratios to plants and animals for estimating the number of species on Earth. There is typically agreement among them over species numbers of higher taxonomic groups such as mammals, birds and reptiles. There is understandably a lot of disagreement over the numbers of insects, fungi and other microbial species.

Today there are 8–20 million species of eukaryotes, maybe many more. In addition, there are unknown and much larger numbers of archaea and bacteria, which do not have a cell nucleus, called 'prokaryotes'. Our lack of knowledge is enormous. Fewer than 2 million species of eukaryotes have been recognised and named so far but even that number is contested, as species in the samples that were previously judged to have been different are sometimes found on re-examination to have been the same. The most systematically and intensively studied are insects (class Insecta), which comprise nearly 60 per cent of all named species.

Biodiversity has several dimensions that look below and above that of species. Genes combine to form organisms, organisms are grouped into species, species combine to form assemblages of populations called guilds, and guilds combine to form communities that interact with the physical world to form ecosystems. At a minimum, biodiversity means the diversity of species and the genes that combine to form the organisms that comprise the species. But the minimum will prove to be too refined for our purposes here, for if we are concerned with Nature's supply of her goods and services, we need to include *ecosystems* and *their* diversity, not only species and their diversity. A landscape that has been given over entirely to modern agriculture is no doubt productive in crop output, but it is poor in supplying other provisioning goods (timber, clean water, pharmaceuticals), never mind maintenance and regulating services.

The energy that primary producers (for example, photosynthesising plants) capture from the Sun, along with the nutrients and other non-living materials they deploy, flow through ecosystems as processes that give rise to Nature's regeneration. We should therefore expect biodiversity in an ecosystem to be a factor in its ability to supply Nature's goods and services. But what we will call an ecosystem's productivity (we could also call it its health) should be seen not only in its average production of goods and services, but also in its resilience to shocks imparted by extreme events, for overly fragile ecosystems would not last long. Biodiversity strengthens an ecosystem's processes. The influence is mutual, for ecosystem processes support biodiversity. That mutual influence enables Nature to renew constantly. This is supported by evidence collated by the ecologists Paul Ehrlich and Peter Raven, which showed that co-evolution between plants and butterflies may have contributed to diversification among both plants and butterflies. And that again points to the importance of species' population size. Diversity is of little moment if there are only a few of each. As Fig. 1.1 shows, if the population size of a species is small, it is unlikely to survive.

An ecosystem's productivity thus depends less on the diversity of species of plants, animals and microorganisms that exist within it than on them performing particular functions and on their population size. The biodiversity in a wetland that filters water effectively differs from the biodiversity needed in a woodland that supplies timber, which in turn differs from the biodiversity in a grassland that supports wildlife. So, a mere headcount of species would be a poor index of biodiversity. Nearly all the organisms that help to produce an ecosystem's goods and services are hidden from view – a gram of soil may contain as many as 10 billion bacterial cells. That may be why those organisms are usually missing in popular programmes about the natural world, which most often inform us of the habits and practices of charismatic animal species and the perils they face today.

A large body of work involving field experiments, site studies and aerial surveys, complemented by mathematical modelling, has found that the number of functional groups in an ecosystem – that is, functional diversity – is strongly related to the productivity of ecosystems as measured by the maintenance and regulating services they provide. Functional diversity points to complementarities among traits, akin to complementarities among the maintenance and regulating services that are provided by ecosystems. The ecologist David Tilman and his collaborators have also found that functional diversity is a determinant of the efficiency with which an ecosystem uses nutrients such as nitrogen and phosphorus.

Drawing an analogy with human society, we could say (functional) biodiversity in an ecosystem resembles the diversity of human talents in an economy needed for it to thrive. Or to use the language of finance: just as diversity within a financial portfolio reduces risk and uncertainty in yield, biodiversity increases an ecosystem's resilience to shocks, and reduces risks to the goods and services it produces. And drawing on an analogy with industrial products in modern societies, biodiversity provides ecosystems with spare parts; it enables ecosystems to be resilient, to be able to adapt to changing circumstances, and to be productive. A healthy ecosystem harbours small populations of species that are waiting in the wings and would increase in numbers if a dominant species were to suffer decline owing to changing circumstances. Reduce biodiversity, and the productivity of ecosystems suffers.

In soil, for instance, different groups of organisms act to maintain soil health in different ways. Archaea, bacteria and fungi act as chemical engineers, decomposing plant residues and soil organic matter, contributing to the transfer of nutrients and the recovery of polluted soils. Other organisms act as biological regulators, controlling plant pathogens and contributing to food security. Larger organisms, such as earthworms, termites and small mammals, act as ecosystem engineers, controlling the structure of the soil matrix. Experiments with soil biodiversity have shown that plant diversity, their decomposition following death and the recycling of nutrients are impaired when the diversity and abundance of various groups of soil biota (fungi, bacteria and nematodes) are reduced. Without these diverse species playing different roles, the soil would fail to support the global food system. Mutual dependence among the species is a reason diversity enhances the health of ecosystems.

Mutual dependency among the species, each contributing to others' fitness to survive, enhances the health of ecosystems. For instance, large fruit-eating vertebrates disperse the seeds of trees in tropical forests. Such animals are, however, a favourite food source of predators, and studies have found that a decline in their populations substantially reduces the carbon-storage potentials of large trees in the forest.

In food webs, the relationships between populations affecting the state of an ecosystem are unidirectional. In oceans, primary producers like phytoplankton and seaweeds are at the bottom of the food chain, while species higher up consume those that are below. Species whose impact on a community structure is large relative to their size and abundance, called keystones, are usually at the top end of the food chain. If these keystone species drop in abundance, there is the potential for species lower in the food chain, previously controlled by the keystones, to explode in numbers, extinguishing local competitors, and their consumers, and causing the ecosystem to cascade into a different state.

Sea otters are an example. They feed on a variety of invertebrates, such as abalone and sea urchins. More than a century ago, excessive hunting for their fur on the west coast of the United States brought the otter population to near extinction. This led to an explosion in the population of sea urchins, which in turn meant the depletion of kelp forests, as sea urchins devour kelp. But kelp are primary producers, creating a habitat in the marine environment for diverse assemblages of marine life, including fin fish. The reintroduction of otters into areas from which they had been eradicated helped to regenerate the kelp forests and restore equilibrium to the ecosystem. This and other examples tell us that populations of species shape habitats not only through mutual interactions as in food webs, but also indirectly, by pollinating, dispersing seeds, fertilising the soil and decomposing detritus.

Species–Area Relationships

From the time humans evolved, our dependency on biodiversity has remained complete. Indeed, we ourselves are a part of biodiversity. But attempts to preserve biodiversity directly would in most cases be a non-starter because we would not know with any accuracy what species were lost, nor where they resided. There are 45,000 recorded species of mites alone, but there may perhaps be 1 million more; around 25,000 recorded species of nematodes and possibly 500,000 more; 100,000 fungi, and possibly some 2.2 to 3.8 million more. There is vast uncertainty in these numbers. Moreover, unlike habitats, species numbers cannot be observed directly. It is not possible to place bounds on species extinction rates when the number of species lies within such large ranges.

In contrast, habitat destruction *can* be witnessed and verified. The ecologists Stuart Pimm and Peter Raven have observed that many species found across large areas of any given habitat reside in small areas within it. That means habitat losses initially may cause few extinctions, but the numbers of extinctions would then be expected to rise as the last remnants of a habitat are destroyed. At current rates of habitat destruction, the peak of extinctions may not occur for a long while, perhaps even decades.

Because we know that species reside in their habitats and we can observe and measure the size of an area, conservation measures on habitats can serve as a substitute for biodiversity conservation. But is an area's size related to the number of species it harbours? If it is, what might the relationship be?

Imagine, first, as a thought experiment, that Earth's surface is a repetitive pattern. The number of species in an area would then be constant, independent of the area's size. Populations of species would be larger in larger areas, but their proportions would on average be the same. However, as habitats differ across space, species differ across space. The influence, as we have already noted, is mutual: the more habitats, the more species; the more species, the more habitats. Consider, then, an ecosystem that is not unsettled by large external disturbances. If the variety of habitats in the ecosystem is found to increase with area, we would predict, even without looking for evidence, that the number of species increases with the size of the area. But in which way?

We would expect the relationship, if there is one, to differ across species and habitat characteristics. As no one could count all species, we must be a lot more specific – for example, we could study the number of species of vascular plants in habitats of different sizes in an aspen forest. Ideally, the tactic would be to include more and more adjacent areas to an initial forest plot and track the number of additional numbers of species of vascular plants in the adjacent areas to see if there is a link between the number of species and the size of the area.

In forests, plants compete for sunlight and water. And there are local variations in soil quality. The result is a distribution of plants in which a relatively small number of large trees and a larger number of medium-sized trees proportionately take up much of the scarce resources, while an even larger numbers of small trees, shrubs and grasses fill in the cracks. It has been found that, as a reasonable approximation, the spatial configuration of large, medium and small tree species in forests resembles the spatial configuration of branches in oak trees or that of coastlines (where the whole is made up of smaller components that have the same pattern or shape as the whole), in that the configurations appear to be self-similar at all discernible scales. Self-similar configurations are known as fractals. In a forest, self-similarity means that the ratio of a proportional increase in the number of tree species in an area associated with a proportional increase in the size of that area is the same no matter whether that area is $100km^2$ or $1,000km^2$. We call that constant ratio the 'scale factor'. As you would expect, the numerical value of the scale factor depends on the species and the characteristics of the forest.

There are many field studies reporting the relationships between numbers of species and the size of the areas they inhabit. For birds, ants and plants in the ecosystems that have been studied, the scale factor has been found to be in the region of 0.2 to 0.8. As illustration, suppose the value of the scale factor is 0.5 for an area of forest. If the area is deforested, so that it is now a quarter of the size it was previously,

Fractals can be observed throughout nature; a romanesco broccoli, for instance, is made up of smaller components resembling the whole (Nature Picture Library)

we would expect half the species in the original area to have become extinct. Therein lies the value of species–area relationships: they allow us to infer the loss of biodiversity from declines in natural habitats.

Fig. 2.1 is an example of the relationship between species numbers and the area where the species have their habitats. It shows that the number of species increases with area, but that it does so less than proportionately, meaning that the scale factor is less than 1. The curvature of the species–area curve faces downward because the number of species has an upper limit set by the total number of species at the largest scale, which is the biosphere. So, as you increase the size of the area in your study, more and more of the species you detect will have been counted already, which means you

FIG. 2.1 RELATIONSHIP BETWEEN NUMBER OF
SPECIES AND THE AREA OF HABITAT

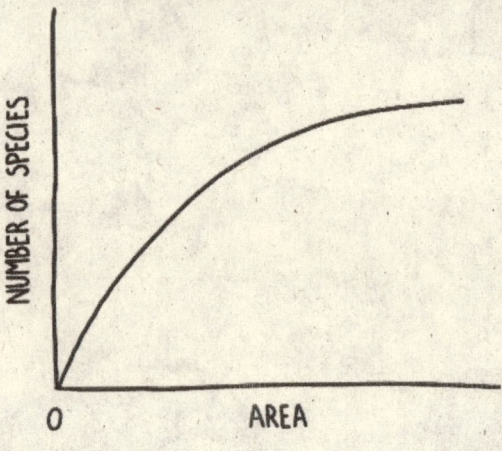

are adding smaller and smaller numbers of species in your samples with each additional area.

Species Conservation or Habitat Protection?

Human-induced habitat destruction is today the leading cause of species extinction. If we want to reduce species extinctions, never mind reduce declines in functional bio-diversity, we should set limits on habitat destruction. Species–area relationships are useful for addressing this. As an illustration, here is a rough estimate of extinctions that can be expected from the continuing destruction of tropical rainforests, this time with bird species in mind.

Of the approximately 10,000 bird species today, some 5,000 inhabit tropical rainforests. We may reasonably assume from field studies that the scale factor in the species–area relationship is a conservative 0.25. Suppose a further 50 per cent of tropical forests were destroyed in the next 100 years. It would mean a loss of about 13 per cent of bird species there, or 650 species. Other things being equal, the extinction of 650 species of birds in 100 years out of a total of 10,000 species of birds yields a figure of 650 extinctions per million species per year. The rate of species extinctions over the past million years or so, called the 'background rate', was 0.1 to 1 extinction per million species per year. So, 650 extinctions per million species per year corresponds to either 65 times or 650 times the background rate, depending on whether that rate is taken to be 0.1 or 1 extinction per million species per year.

Suppose, however, that humanity can come to grips with species extinction and limits tropical deforestation to only a further 0.8 per cent over the next 100 years. That would mean an eventual extinction of 0.1 per cent of bird species, that is, 10 species. Even that is 10 or 100 times the background extinction rate, depending on whether that extinction rate per million species per year is taken to be 0.1 or 1. Obviously, destruction of tropical rainforests will have to come to a complete halt if the extinction rates of birds are to be brought down to anything like the background rates of species extinction. And we have not accounted for the millions of other uncounted species that are being extinguished in those forests and elsewhere.

Biodiversity is essential to the health of ecosystems, and ecosystems are assets of vital importance to the human economy. Species–area relationships explain why habitat conservation is essential for maintaining biodiversity. But, as always, there are exceptions to the rule that the reasoning should proceed from habitat conservation to the implied conservation of species. For charismatic species, the reasoning would run the other way. We will, for example, want to protect the habitats of the gorillas of Rwanda because we want to protect gorillas from extinction, and it is the gorillas that have drawn our attention to the forests they inhabit.

CHAPTER 3
Human Impact in the Past

Humans, like other species, leave an imprint of their activities on the biosphere. Some call it our (ecological) 'impact', others call it our ecological 'footprint', and we will use the terms interchangeably. Our direct demands are for provisioning goods, so, our footprint leaves a visible imprint on the state of the ecosystems on which we make our demands. The imprint of slash-and-burn agriculture, for example, is a time-old marker; the resulting plot is called a swidden, which when left fallow soon gets covered by shrubs and stunted trees. But there is a *hidden* imprint of our activities: the imprint on maintenance and regulating services. Alter the character of an ecosystem, and the composition of the maintenance and regulating services it offers changes. We have already established that provisioning goods and maintenance and regulating services are tied to one another: if one is compromised, so is the other. We have also seen that biodiversity, suitably identified, offers a measure of the health of ecosystems and their ability to supply provisioning goods.

We began by considering the biodiversity losses that follow changes in our use of land, such as when we convert forests, grasslands, wetlands and peatbogs into farmland, plantations, roads, towns and cities. These examples could lead us to think that our footprint in the distant past was negligible but is now large because of our greater numbers and increased skills. If we look closer at our activities, though, we find that there are reasons to question our assumption about our negligible impact in the past (but we will confirm the assumption about the present in the next chapter).

Humanity's closest relatives, a group we call hominids, make their appearance in the fossil record in Africa at the start of the Pleistocene (sometimes known as the 'Ice Age', the most recent of several ice ages), about 2.7 million years ago. This was an epoch of repeated glaciations, the latest of which ended some 12,000 years ago, at the beginning of what is called the Holocene epoch. One of those hominids, *Homo erectus*, was the first to migrate out of Africa to the north, around 2 million years ago, where it, along with Neanderthals, Denisovans and the few other species that had evolved in the north, represented humanity until the occurrence of another significant migration out of Africa. That event occurred at least 60,000 years ago, when hominids present in Eurasia were joined by *Homo sapiens*, or modern humans, who had originated in Africa about 200,000 years ago. By about 40,000 years ago, the other hominids in Eurasia were extinct.*

---

* The broad reason for their extinction is that they were at a competitive disadvantage against *Homo sapiens* in exploiting natural resources. There are refinements of this. Some anthropologists argue that modern humans moved in larger and less isolated groups, and developed more advanced tools and skills in consequence. There is also evidence that

For tens of thousands of years after *Homo sapiens* reached Eurasia, they lived as hunter-gatherers. Fossil deposits of bones, teeth, shells and stone tools, together with studies of social structures among contemporary hunter-gatherers, suggest the basic social units were bands of 20 to 50 individuals, moving periodically from place to place, and meeting seasonally with others in the same kinship group. (The fossil record of injured skeletons also suggests that encounters among different kinship groups were not infrequently violent.) Over the millennia, *Homo sapiens* learned to create artistic works and make weapons and musical instruments, but because they were frequently on the move in search of food, there was little opportunity for them to develop what we today call civilisation.

The intercontinental migration of *Homo sapiens* took place during the last glacial period, when the sea level fell and exposed land bridges. Human migration from Eurasia to Australia (about 40,000–50,000 years ago) occurred long before there was any domestication of plants and animals. Dispersal to North America (via the then existing Bering Land Bridge connecting northern Siberia and Alaska) occurred some 18,000 years ago (possibly even earlier), after the domestication of dogs (more than 20,000 years ago), which they brought with them.

Neanderthals and Denisovans were unable to adapt their hunting methods to compete against *Homo sapiens* when large tracts in Eurasia changed into sparsely vegetated steppes and semi-desert during the last ice age. To that we add the traditional explanation, which is the violence *Homo sapiens* inflicted on Neanderthals and Denisovans, but not before interbreeding with them during their encounters.

In addition to the extinction of other hominids, the period following *Homo sapiens*'s move out of Africa also saw the large-scale extinction of megafauna in Eurasia of a magnitude unprecedented in millions of years, and extinctions in Australia and the Americas followed the dispersals of modern humans there too. The process had begun earlier in Eurasia – the archaeological records point to 120,000 years ago – but it accelerated with the arrival of *Homo sapiens*.

There is evidence that *Homo sapiens* were the prime movers of the extinction. Megafauna carnivores were competitors for game and were also a physical threat, while megafauna herbivores competed directly against human foragers for plant food and were themselves fodder. Megafauna were also sources of hide, bones and tusks. Human bands used fire to flush animals out, corral them or catch them with nets, and kill them using stone tools.

African megafauna, however, did not suffer that fate. Why? The received explanation is that humans had co-evolved with African animals; each knew the other's ways. Hunting them was costly, in effort, time and lives. In contrast, *Homo sapiens* were strangers to the megafauna in Eurasia, even more so to those in the Americas and Australia. They did not fear the strangers because they had no instinctive reason to fear them. In effect, they were a sitting target for human assaults.*

---

* As elsewhere in the social sciences, simple explanations should be treated with suspicion. We are considering megafauna numbers over the long period of the last ice age when habitats were undergoing changes under climatic pressure. Some experts believe that populations

The extinction of megafauna resulted in cascading effects on the composition of plant communities, vegetation structure and ecosystem functions. Novel communities that had waited in the wings emerged and fires increased in frequency. But the process of ecological change was slow enough for early humans to adapt to them. As hunter-gatherers, they were in any case always on the move to find more habitable environments.

Why did *Homo sapiens* hunt the megafauna to extinction and not conserve them as stocks of natural capital? The reason is that the animals were not for them to conserve. The giant animals, not all that fleet of foot, were 'open access resources', for no band of *Homo sapiens* owned any of them. That meant the bands had every incentive to hunt them down on encountering them on their continual journeys. Fortunately, there were also smaller fauna to be hunted, but even though they were also open access resources, they couldn't be hunted to extinction. Being smaller in size, they bred more frequently, were larger in numbers, and were fleet of foot or wing. Because the cost of snaring small fauna was high and the human population was small, the animals could endure.

The atmosphere, the open seas and biodiversity writ large are global public goods, essential for our existence, never mind our wellbeing. In this regard they are unlike the megafauna of the Pleistocene. But they resemble the megafauna of that distant past in one crucial respect: they are open access resources. To be sure, they have always been open

---

of megafauna in Eurasia and the Americas were already reduced in size. The arrival of humans, it is thought, merely finished the job.

access resources; but in the Pleistocene, it didn't matter, for humans were few and their tools were primitive; hardly any even reached the open seas. Today, we humans are so large in numbers and have created such powerful technologies that, unless we take collective action, those public goods will go the way of the megafauna of the Pleistocene – not literally, of course, but they will change in character so drastically and so rapidly that we in all probability won't be able to adapt to the changes.

The impact of humans on Nature continued with the domestication of plants and animals. Cattle were domesticated in southwest Anatolia and the Near East some 8,500–10,000 years ago, and the breeding of horses in captivity began at least 5,000 years ago, maybe even earlier, in the grasslands of the western steppe. The wheel was invented around the same time, the combination of horses and wheeled carts enabling pastoralists to travel, carrying their way of life to distant places. Pastoralism led to large-scale deforestation and a corresponding loss in biodiversity. Migrations of pastoralists, herding horses and cattle, began a transformation of the landscape that accelerated with the introduction of crop agriculture.

Farming was discovered in a period of rising temperatures following the last ice age, with crops beginning to be cultivated some 12,000 years ago in the Fertile Crescent of the Middle East, a region that includes the Tigris and Euphrates rivers. (Both in North and South America, crop agriculture was developed independently and a few millennia later.) Along with domesticated animals, cultivated crops provided a major source of storable food, one that could see humans through droughts, winters and other unfavourable times. At that time, the global population is thought by paleo-historians to have been about 1 million people, with only about 100,000 in Europe. Agriculture, however, allowed a single person to feed more than themselves and their family, and made possible a rapid increase in population. Farmers from the Fertile Crescent swept into Europe, displacing the sparse population that had existed there earlier.

In cultivated lands, the numbers of people who could live together in a village, town or city increased greatly. The first cities were built in southern Mesopotamia between the Tigris and Euphrates rivers some 7,000 years ago. The economic surplus enabled most aspects of what we call civilisation to develop there. Individuals could learn to become toolmakers, soldiers, tradesmen and priests, and the various elements of what we consider to be civilisation began to develop.

As our human numbers grew, our impact on the planet increased. By about 3,000 years ago, pastoralists, agriculturists and hunter-gatherers had transformed large areas as they grouped together and grew food for their increasing numbers. So, human-induced ecological transformations are not a modern phenomenon; what is different today is the unprecedented speed and magnitude of those changes.

Deep Economic History

If human history is a mere blink in the story of the biosphere, economic history in turn is a tiny fraction of that.

Drawing on material objects uncovered from archaeological sites, sketches of quantitative history reach about 5,000 years into the past, but quantitative *economic* history looks back at best to the start of the Common Era (CE).

The economist Angus Maddison spent much of his professional life uncovering past living standards across the world. To do that, he chose GDP per capita as a measure of the standard of living in a society, because it is the index in most common use today for assessing the performance of economies and for evaluating macroeconomic policy. GDP is the market value of the flow of all final goods and services produced within a country in a year. It includes the market value of aggregate private consumption, or consumer spending, gross investment (including the capital expenditures of businesses), the sum of government expenditures, and the difference between exports and imports. GDP is a measure of an economy's aggregate output. As the value of output must reach *someone's* pocket, we will use the terms 'output' and 'income' interchangeably.

Peering into the past 2,000 years with a measuring rod, which is what Maddison did, requires gumption, as one must search for data that would fit one's requirements for the task, and it is not obvious what those data are nor where they are to be found. But Maddison used whatever record he could find that gave clues to wages, food consumption, clothing, housing, land rents and so on. Table 3.1 presents the estimates of global per capita GDP from year 1 CE to 2019 (the year before the wider COVID outbreak), constructed from ongoing work by others in what is now known as the Maddison Project.

TABLE 3.1: PER CAPITA GLOBAL GDP FROM I CE, IN DOLLARS PPP (PURCHASING POWER PARITY) AT 2011 PRICES

Year:	I	1000	1500	1700	1820	1900	1950	2000	2019
$:	745	725	900	980	1,135	2,450	3,280	9,455	15,980

Source: Maddison Project Data Base (2020)

You'll notice that over a long stretch, until about 1500 CE, the global living standard was pretty much stagnant, rising slowly from then until the start of the Industrial Revolution, growing somewhat more rapidly from then, and taking a sharp and accelerated increase from around the middle of the twentieth century.

You can also notice that the average person was very poor right up to the beginning of the modern period (around about 1700 CE). In Late Antiquity and the Middle Ages, global average income was not much above 1.90 dollars a day – a figure that was taken by the World Bank in 2015 to be the threshold of extreme poverty.

Table 3.1 hides social improvements taking place in the 1,700 years following Year 1 in various parts of the world. An interval of a thousand years (1–1000 CE) hides fluctuations of fortunes in different regions. But historical records do not point to sustained improvements in living standards in any region in that period. For example, the economic historian Peter Temin has suggested that per capita GDP in the Roman Empire in the second century CE was about the same as in India in 1990. But in time the empire fell, and incomes dropped. We also know of the Black Death and Europe's revival after it, both of which are hidden from view in the broad 500-year spell between 1000 and 1500 CE. Despite the caveats, though, the pioneering Maddison estimates of per capita GDP in deep economic history are a stark reminder that for nearly all of history the average person in the world was extremely poor.

Fig. 3.1, constructed from Table 3.1, gives a visual account of the global living standard since the Industrial Revolution, approximately 1750 CE. Notice that the rise in per

FIG 3.1 REAL GDP PER CAPITA

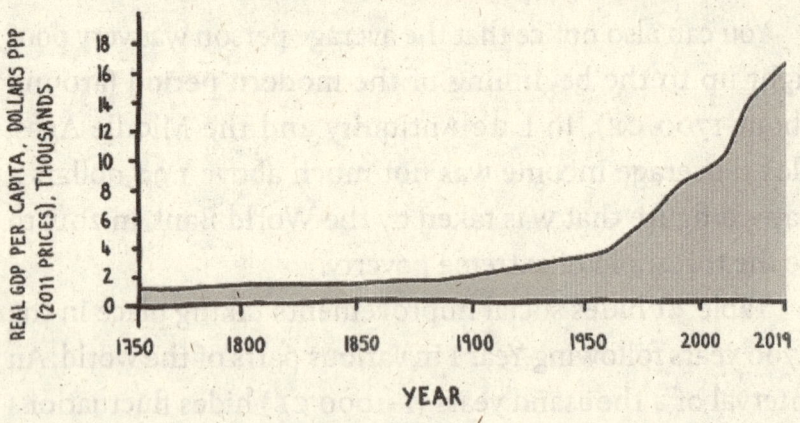

SOURCE: DASGUPTA (2021, 2024)

capita GDP began in 1900, and it rose even more sharply as recently as 1950.

The Malthusian Thesis

At the very end of the eighteenth century, the Rev. Thomas Malthus published *An Essay on the Principle of Population*, where he suggested that population size and the standard of living had kept each other in check throughout history in what we would today call a low-level equilibrium. The world at that time was composed largely of organic economies, where not only food but also most raw materials needed for manufacturing were either animal or plant in origin. To expand food production, farmers ploughed ever more inferior land, an exercise in diminishing returns. Given the reproductive norms of societies (although this is not quite how Malthus put it), a population grew whenever living standards rose above the equilibrium level, bringing living standards down. But whenever living standards fell below the equilibrium level, more people died, and the system equilibrated. As a matter of common observation, the (equilibrium) living standard was low, as Table 3.1 confirms.

Both population and living standards in Malthus's theory, like any good theory, were determined by factors operating at a deeper level. So, he identified various possible causes that had perturbed economies throughout history (wars and the vagaries of Nature were two proximate drivers) from which they returned to equilibrium. Table 3.2 and the corresponding Fig. 3.2 present estimates of global population from 1 to 2023 CE. Population barely rose in the first millennium CE and in 1500 CE was not even double that in 1 CE. A serious and sustained rise in global population has taken place only since 1820 CE, sometime after Malthus published his classic. But even that rise was trivial compared to what has happened since 1950.

TABLE 3.2: GLOBAL POPULATION FROM 1 CE (MILLIONS)

Year:	1	1000	1500	1760	1820	1900	1950	2000	2023
Population:	230	270	450	770	1,000	1,600	2,500	6,100	8,100

Source: Maddison Project Data Base (2020)

FIG. 3.2 GLOBAL POPULATION FROM YEAR 1 CE

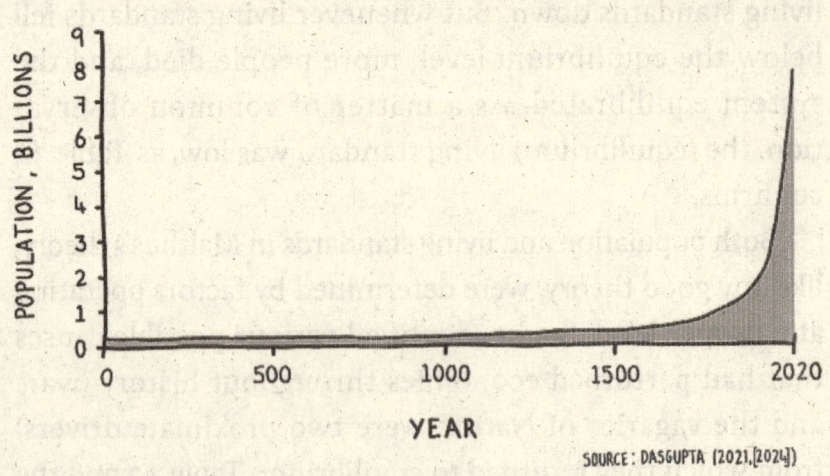

SOURCE: DASGUPTA (2021,[2024])

If we combine the estimates in Figs 3.1 and 3.2, we obtain Fig. 3.3, which gives us an idea of the pace with which the size of the global economy (global GDP) has increased since 1750. Once again, 1950 is found to have been a watershed.

Of course, income is only one factor in evaluating the standard of living. Another measure, prominently used today, is life expectancy at birth. Table 3.3 presents the estimates of that from 1 to 2023 CE. What is striking is how flat it was until a bit after 1900 (it remained within the range 24–31 years). Unsafe drinking water, infectious diseases and periodic crop failures kept child mortality high, thus life expectancy low. Life expectancy began to increase only after

FIG. 3.3 GLOBAL GDP FROM 1750 CE

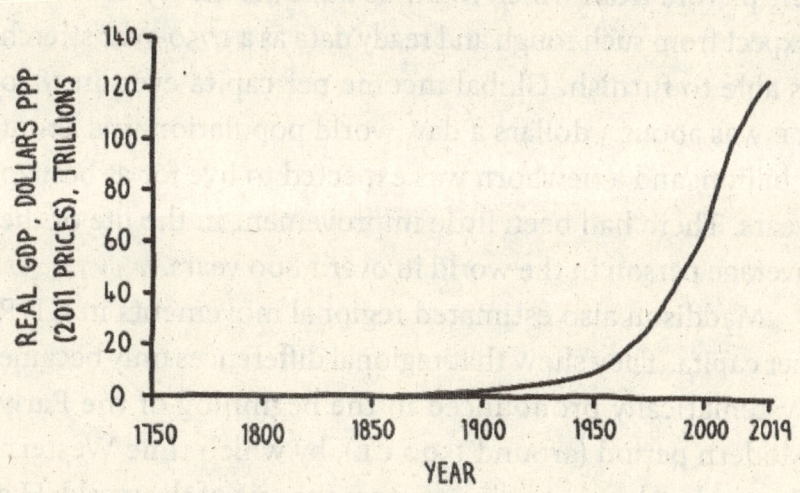

SOURCE: DASGUPTA (2021,(2024))

65

1900 and, with improvements in public hygiene, access to potable water and the discovery of antibiotics, rose sharply after 1950.

TABLE 3.3: LIFE EXPECTANCY AT BIRTH FROM I CE

Year:	I	1000	1500	1760	1820	1900	1950	2000	2023
Age:	24	24	24	25	29	31	46	66	73

Source: Adapted from Dasgupta (2021, [2024])

Taken together, these figures suggest that the global experience until about 1750 CE was pretty much in line with Malthus's observations. Certainly, they are as good a fit to the picture from which Malthus built his theory as we can expect from such rough and ready data as a 1,750-year stretch is able to furnish. Global income per capita even in 1820 CE was about 3 dollars a day, world population was about 1 billion, and a newborn was expected to live for at best 30 years. There had been little improvement in the life of the average person in the world in over 1,800 years.

Maddison also estimated regional movements in GDP per capita. They show that regional differences only became systematically pronounced in the beginning of the Early Modern period (around 1500 CE), by which time Western Europe had begun to diverge from the rest of the world. His estimates suggest that even in 1700 CE the average person in Asia languished in near-extreme poverty, at around 2.5

dollars a day (at 2011 prices). As tourists we are dazzled by the art, architecture and technology of past eras. We refer to them as great civilisations and imagine that those must have been prosperous times as well. The evidence says we should imagine otherwise. So long as there is a ruling class to tax poor subjects, we have the beginning of the arts, humanities and the sciences. The Taj Mahal, for example, which is today the most renowned construction of the Early Modern era, was built in the mid-seventeenth century on the orders of a tyrant in memory of his favourite wife, on the backs of extremely poor subjects. Great art, great architecture, great literature and even great discoveries about the natural world can coexist with general squalor and widespread deprivation of the means available for a reasonable existence. And they have coexisted for nearly all of history. Average world income in 1820 CE was only about 50 per cent higher than in 1 CE.

While Malthus's theory would appear to have described the global economy well in 1798, the year in which he published his work, it had already begun to unravel in relation to Europe from, many historians believe, as early as the sixteenth century, with the seeds having been laid even earlier. There was a growing difference between Europe and the rest of the world. For example, China was technologically superior to Europe in 1500 CE, having invented paper, gunpowder, printing and the compass among other technologies. But maritime trade was stopped by imperial decree around 1500, and the country subsequently became inward looking and fell behind.

Identifying the factors that led to the great divergence between Europe and the rest of the world has been a major subject of research among scholars studying deep economic history. It is not in contention that a series of societal changes took place in Europe in the Early Modern period (perhaps even earlier), which unleashed the forces of innovation that account for the emergence of the modern world. The physicist Steven Weinberg has gone even further to make the case that the way we practise science is itself a European discovery. The idea of the Scientific Revolution of the sixteenth and seventeenth centuries was not put forward without basis; the debate has been over the factors underlying the divergence between Europe and the rest of the world and its timing.

Many contemporary historians point to the exploitation, including the practice of the enslavement, and even obliteration of non-European societies as the route European powers took to make their own societies rich, and subsequently enrich the societies they established in the western offshoots (North America, Australia, New Zealand). True no doubt, but it somewhat begs a question; it doesn't explain why Europe gained the upper hand when it did, nor why the exploitation wasn't the other way round; why, say, the Aztecs didn't invade Spain and enslave its people in the sixteenth century, or why the Ottomans couldn't take over much of Europe, or why the Arabs, who had practised slavery even earlier, were unable to build on the technological skills they acquired in their Golden Age, 750–1250 CE, to conquer the whole of Europe.

The historian David Landes identified several societal factors underlying Europe's advance and noted that in the Early Modern era the continent was not a monolithic state.

Rivalry, competition and differences in power and beliefs among dukes, princes and clerical eminences enabled ideas to flourish. If a scientist was in disfavour in one state, he (it was always a 'he') could find service in a rival court.

The Industrial Revolution (1750 or thereabouts, although the date is a mere marker) that followed the Scientific Revolution unleashed growth in labour productivity from technological advances and the production scale economies that came with those advances. By the beginning of the twentieth century, Malthus's theory began to unravel elsewhere too, barring Asia (Japan excluded) and Africa. By then, as Tables 3.1–3.3 show, the global population had risen to 1.6 billion, life expectancy at birth had advanced to 31 years, and average income had grown to more than 2,000 international dollars a year.

None of that success, however, was accompanied by the institutional changes that were needed to protect the environment. Technological advancements were directed at making mining and harvesting cheaper, with little regard for the environmental damage that came with those activities. Labour- and capital-saving devices, not Nature-saving devices, were the entrepreneur's goal. Economies of scale were sought to make the unit cost of production low; there was little attention paid to the havoc large-scale industrial production would inflict on the natural environment.

There were complaints, of course, especially from within the Romantic artistic and intellectual movement of the late eighteenth century, which revered Nature and beauty beyond the rationalism of the Enlightenment and increasing economic materialism. They pointed to the damages industrial pollution was inflicting on local communities. Today, we would say those damages should be added to the idea of production costs, but no economist of the nineteenth century made the connection.

Maddison's work tells us that even the Industrial Revolution was a prelude to real economic betterment for the average person. Significant increases in the standard of living took place only in the twentieth century, mostly in the West and its western offshoots, and mostly in the latter half of the century. In a matter of 70 years (1950 to 2020), per capita GDP increased more than seven-fold in Western Europe. Which may be why many people are convinced that trade and investment and the economies of scale and technological progress they give rise to can be relied upon to overcome environmental problems. Today, Malthus, the 'pessimistic parson', is seen by some as a 'false prophet', remaining as wrong as ever.[*]

Social commentators have been known to dismiss even deep insights in the social sciences when they do not support desired beliefs. Malthus's insight was that societies routinely experience an imbalance between the demands they make of the biosphere and the biosphere's ability to meet those demands, and that the corrective mechanism societies deploy without any central guidance involves population. When times are bad, population declines, making fewer demands on the biosphere; but when times improve, population increases and brings back bad times. Formally speaking,

* *The Economist*, 15 May 2008.

population adjustment is taken by Mathus to be the mechanism by which a society 'equilibrates'.

Malthus is dismissed by modern commentators because he thought that the mechanism for correcting that imbalance keeps societies in poverty. But as we show below, the imbalance has taken a new expression in the contemporary world. Whether that new expression is 'Malthusian' is of little moment; what *is* of moment is that population increase has been a factor in the current imbalance.

CHAPTER 4

The Impact Inequality

Timescales in the geological sciences differ from those in economics by orders of magnitude (a geological epoch, such as the Pleistocene, which is smaller than an eon, era or period, nevertheless can cover up to tens of millions of years, while an economic period might cover just a few decades). The disciplines ask very different questions and deploy vastly different conceptual tools to address them. To the best of my knowledge, there has been until recently no instance when findings in the two have spoken to one another. There is one now.

The post-war period has been unprecedented in terms of human wellbeing as judged by the measure in most common use (Fig. 3.1). This has excited economic commentators, many of whom have published essays and books to celebrate the fact that the average person in the world has never had it so good. But in a now classic paper of 2016 in the journal *Science*, prominent Earth scientists led by Colin Waters of the British Geological Survey reviewed stratigraphic markers (i.e., markers found in strata or rock layers) in the soils, lakes, seabed and ice cores over the past 12,000 years (the Holocene) and found an abrupt change in the middle of the last century: suddenly there were large deposits of metals, pesticides, concrete, nitrogen, plastics, phosphorus and aluminium, as well as concentrations of carbon dioxide and methane, in the soil, seabed and water. The authors suggested that the mid-twentieth century (1950, to make the onset instantly recallable) should be regarded as marking the beginning of a sharp rise in human activities within what can be called the 'Anthropocene' to reflect that we are now living in a human-dominated planet. Earth scientists tend to report their findings in deadpan prose, but the subtext of the *Science* article spoke of a dark present.

The appearance of dissonance between the two sets of findings is illusory. The article in *Science* reported abrupt changes in the composition of natural capital, which corresponded with abrupt improvements in our standard of living. The latter set of statistics don't say whether the improvements in living standards were achieved by depreciating natural capital, but the article in *Science* tells us that they did, for the improvements came in tandem with a severely polluted Earth.

The stratigraphic signatures in the *Science* article were deposits of industrial material. What are their ecological counterparts? The Millennium Ecosystem Assessment (MEA) of 2005 found that 15 of the 24 ecosystem services assessed (ranging from provisioning goods such as food, water and timber, to regulating services that affect climate and disease, to cultural services such as recreational spiritual benefits, and maintenance services such as soil formation) were in decline. In turn, building on the work of MEA, a global assessment by the Intergovernmental Platform on Biodiversity and Ecosystem Services (IPBES), published in 2019, reported that Nature's goods and services in 14 of 18 categories have suffered a decline since 1970.

The International Union for Conservation of Nature (IUCN), based in Gland, Switzerland, in 2014 compiled a list of endangered ecosystems, called a Red List.* IUCN's list and the two global assessments fall squarely in line with the rise in human activities in recent decades. Since the 1970s, some 20–35 per cent of mangrove forests globally have been destroyed for their timber or to accommodate urban expansion, coastal population growth and increasing numbers of shrimp farms. A quarter of all tropical forests have been destroyed since the Convention on Biological Diversity was ratified in Rio de Janeiro in 1992. We also deposit more nitrogen compounds into terrestrial and marine ecosystems today than are generated in the natural nitrogen cycle (more than 100 million tons of fertilisers are used annually in agriculture). Soil acidification, eutrophication of freshwater lakes and marine dead zones are among the consequences of nitrogen and phosphorus overload. Levels of oxygen in the oceans have declined continuously over the past 50 years owing to algae growth. While it is natural to have some low oxygen areas in the seas, the size of these areas has expanded by 4.5 million km² – roughly the size of the European Union – and the volume of water with zero

---

* The list includes collapsed ecosystems, such as the Aral Sea.

oxygen has quadrupled. In coastal waters, the number of sites with low oxygen has risen from 50 to 500, and that is probably an underestimate.*

There is now a huge volume of evidence of human overreach of the biosphere when read in terms of species extinction. Extinction rates in the recent past can be inferred from deploying estimates of changes in land use that have taken place in empirically drawn species–area relationships. For the distant past, this approach is ineffective, as reliable records of changes in land use are unavailable. Extinction rates in the distant past are inferred instead from comparisons with fossil records in groups that have hard body parts (vertebrates and molluscs). Extinction rates in periods separating the five mass extinction events, for example, have been estimated by first examining populations of species in fossils and then identifying those groups of species that are

---

* A closer look at our activities is telling. Net primary production (NPP) is the regeneration rate of primary producers, or the amount of biomass produced by photosynthesisers net of losses through respiration. Primary producers include not only naturally growing plants, algae and many bacteria, but also agricultural and plantation crops. Land on which crops are grown today were once woodlands, forests, grasslands, marshes and wetlands. We may then ask what proportion of the regeneration rate of terrestrial primary producers is usurped by humans. Various estimates put the figure at 20–40 per cent, and at 60–90 per cent in intensively farmed regions, which means we are crowding out other herbivores, and by implication carnivores and omnivores. No doubt global NPP has increased over the decades (some estimate that it has increased by 20 per cent in the past 50 years), but the composition of NPP matters. Agricultural fields and plantations are monocultures, meaning they house little biodiversity.

missing in fossils of a subsequent time. This is inevitably a crude exercise, which is why estimates of extinction rates have error bars covering an order of magnitude.

As mentioned previously, rates of the extinction of species of eukaryotes (which cover everything with membrane-bound nuclei from a single-cell organism to the blue whale) in the past million years or more, called the 'background rate', were 0.1–1 species extinctions per million species per year. That rate has increased alarmingly in the recent past and is now 100 to 1,000 times higher than the background rate.* To illustrate the significance of these numbers, suppose that the extinction rate is currently 1,000 times a background rate of, say, 1 species per million species per year, and that there are 15 million species of eukaryotes. We would then expect 1.5 million species of eukaryotes to become extinct over the next 100 years, which would amount to *10 per cent* of the number of species of eukaryotes. No doubt new species will emerge, but they will do so at a far slower rate.

There are more targeted estimates of species extinction. In a recent survey of population data on nearly 30,000 species of terrestrial vertebrates, Gerardo Ceballos, Paul Ehrlich and Peter Raven estimated the numbers of species that are on the brink of extinction. The authors' criterion was populations with fewer than 1,000 individuals and, by this measure, 515 species are under threat, representing 1.7 per cent of the vertebrates on the authors' survey list. If extinction follows at the same rate in future, the

* Insect extinction rates are a major source of information.

population of terrestrial vertebrates will halve in about 40 years. Assuming all species on the brink have experienced similar trends in the past, the authors estimate that more than 237,000 populations of those species have vanished since 1900.

In another study (by Ceballos and Ehrlich), the authors estimated that of 5,400 genera of terrestrial vertebrates, 73 have become extinct since 1500 CE. The extinction rate in the sample is 35 times higher than expected in the background rate of 1 extinction per million per year, implying that but for humans it would have taken 18,000 years, not 500, for that number of genera to have become extinct. There would be no species extinction crisis, by definition, if every species was reduced to a single viable population, but we would all be dead from the loss of maintenance and regulating services.

The plain truth though is that we wouldn't necessarily know when a habitat's health is being seriously compromised, which is to say, we would not know where its tipping points are. What we *do* know is that when a habitat tips over, populations of species inhabiting it die, and that extinction is irreversible. We may have little idea today of the role a particular species plays in the health of an ecosystem, but we know that we may know more – maybe a lot more – in the future. Because extinction forecloses options that we would have in the future should the species prove to have been valuable, its preservation has an additional value today. That it has an additional value does not depend on our attitude to risk. Conservation expands our future options, and an expansion of options is valuable irrespective of our attitude to risk. Because that additional value is the value of keeping our options open, it is called an 'option value'. The additional value is a reason for giving populations of species a wider berth.

Judged by what is known about relatively well-studied groups (terrestrial vertebrates, plants), some 20 per cent of species could become extinct within the next several decades, perhaps twice as many by the end of the twenty-first century. It is estimated that 84 mammal species have become extinct since 1500, and 32 of those since 1900.

Such high levels of induced extinction place the scale of humanity's presence in the biosphere in perspective. Our enormous economic success in the Anthropocene has come in tandem with a severely diminished Earth. The enormity of the harm we are causing is, of course, not only directed at ourselves; it has deeper ethical significance, which we explore later. Estimates of contemporary extinction rates also tell us why Earth scientists and ecologists say we are witnessing the *sixth* great biological extinction event since life began.

In striking imagery, Paul Ehrlich brought home the inevitability of an eventual collapse of ecosystems from continual species extinction, by asking us to imagine rivets being popped by some mechanism from the wings of an airborne plane. At first, the plane would not be affected much, but as the number of rivets that have been popped increases, the plane becomes less sturdy, until eventually, *at some uncertain number of popped rivets*, the plane crashes to the ground.

Habitat Fragmentation

We tend to think of human-induced species extinction in terms of large-scale changes in land use: forests being transformed into land for crops, animal farms and plantations; grasslands transformed into pastures; mines and quarries ripping apart dense jungles. But there is a more insidious process at work, which is perhaps as powerful; the bit-by-bit fragmentation of ecosystems that accompanies growth in our demand for the biosphere's provisioning goods.

Persistent, incremental encroachment into Nature is insidious because each move seems near harmless: a new bus lane cutting through an ancient orchard here, a mangrove forest sliced to make way for a luxury hotel there, a bat habitat destroyed to make for additional housing in an urban sprawl elsewhere. The orchard will not return, the mangrove forest won't have space to recover its previous glory, and the bat population will die because it has nowhere to go. If at each move human demand is allowed to trump ecological integrity, the landscape that evolves becomes denuded of biodiversity.

When an ecosystem is fragmented into parts, the supply of maintenance and regulating services declines – the supply from the sum of the parts is less than the supply from the previous whole. Abrupt boundaries appear between patches of land within an ecosystem, each with its own species-area curve, and the length of a boundary, called an 'edge', increases through fragmentation of the ecosystem. This leads to what is known as 'edge effect', whereby the greater amount of edge around a habitat, the more likely it is that the habitat, and therefore its related ecosystems, is going to be affected by external shocks. Striking examples of the effects of fragmentation are river systems that are broken up with dams. They destroy the life cycle of fish species, alter the course of rivers and eliminate communities of organisms on site. Habitat fragmentation reduces biodiversity and so impairs ecosystem functions.

Fragmentation hinders dispersal – animals are wary of entering clearings, as they evolved within large, continuous and climatically stable habitats – and has also been found to expose species to harsh environmental conditions, including fires, diseases and invasive species. The result is a reduction in resilience to shocks. In a long-running study of the Amazon rainforest, Thomas Lovejoy, William Laurance and their colleagues found that even large fragments of forest area (100ha) can lose up to 50 per cent of their species in a dozen years. Clearings as narrow as 80m have been found to hinder recolonisation of fragments by birds, insects and tree-dwelling animals. Fragmentation of natural habitats is thus an early-warning sign of biodiversity loss.

Seventy per cent of Earth's remaining forests today are within 1km of the forest's edge. That is fragmentation on a massive scale. Future losses to natural habitats, from extensions of land devoted to agriculture (estimated by some ecologists to be a near 20 per cent increase by 2050), plantations and mines will only make things worse. And that is before we factor in the inevitable increases in the number and sizes of towns and cities and transportation networks.

Economic vs Ecological Productivity

Economists and ecologists do not speak of the productivity of capital in the same way as each other. Industrial agriculture enables us to produce food per hectare at rates unthinkable in the past. But it does so at the cost of functional and species biodiversity. Croplands as far as the eye can see are productive, but they are productive in mono crops and do not house genetic diversity. Land given over to ranching and animal grazing is productive too, but only in terms of sheep and cattle. Plantations of oil palm and soya are also productive, but they are poor in biodiversity, offering fewer maintenance and regulating services. By fracturing forests, they destroy biodiversity in what remains there.

The fields we see today replaced ecosystems that were once, in varying degrees, diverse in species – grasslands, wetlands, woodlands, tropical rainforests, swamps. And agricultural practices themselves cause biodiversity to be lost, both on and off site. Industrial fertilisers, insecticides and pesticides destroy not only insect life but also soil biodiversity and cause even far away estuaries to become dead zones. Tilling and ploughing destroy life in the soil. The demand for food, water, timber, fibres, minerals and the dams that are built to supply water and produce electricity leads us to tear the landscape apart and alter the composition of natural capital in ways that destroy biodiversity. Along with that is loss in the supply of Nature's maintenance and regulating services, which in turn feeds back to reduce the ability of ecosystems to supply provisioning goods, and that calls for further intervention. There is a vicious cycle at work here.

The human economy today can thus be viewed as being engaged in a continuous tussle between the demands for provisioning goods and our need for the biosphere's maintenance and regulating services to sustain natural capital stocks, by which we can continue to reap the benefits of Nature in the long term. Overreach in our demand for provisioning goods is thus an inability of the biosphere to replenish what we have drawn from it. The substitution of produced capital (factories, roads, townships, machines) for diverse forms of natural capital has not only characterised our investment activities but also shaped our conception of economic progress. It should come as no surprise then that the grammar we have created to understand societal progress is misleading.

Climate Change

In the Holocene until the Industrial Revolution some 250 years ago, the atmospheric concentration of the gas carbon dioxide (CO_2) remained largely constant, at about 280 parts per million (ppm) in volume. There was an equilibrium between what was absorbed by land and the seas and what was released into the atmosphere. The process that maintained equilibrium in the atmosphere's carbon concentration came to be called the 'carbon cycle'. It was one of the biosphere's maintenance and regulating services, contributing to the processes that enabled we humans to thrive in the Holocene.

CO_2 in the atmosphere absorbs the infra-red part of the re-radiated solar energy from Earth's surface, and so acts like a blanket for us and other species. Reduce CO_2 concentration and the global climate will become colder on average; increase it and the global climate will become warmer, which is why carbon dioxide is called a greenhouse gas. Average global warming will also be accompanied by more frequent extreme weather events such as storms and heat waves. A stable carbon concentration in the atmosphere in the Holocene until recently meant a stable global climate.

Since the Industrial Revolution, the rate at which humanity has emitted CO_2 into the atmosphere has been beyond the biosphere's ability to recycle it. The amount that cannot be recycled remains in the atmosphere, which means the carbon cycle has been broken. The concentration of CO_2 has risen to about 420ppm today. Fig. 4.1, taken from the UK Meteorological Office's most recent assessment of global climate change, shows the CO_2 concentration in the atmosphere since 1750 CE. It has the curving, hockey-stick shape of global per capita GDP in Fig. 3.1, and so it is the flipside of the good news that was conveyed by that data. Today, the mean global temperature is very nearly 1.5°C above what it was some 250 years ago, a temperature beyond which the global climate could enter a domain whose characteristics remain so hazy as to be alarming.

The idea of getting to net-zero emissions of CO_2 by 2050 was originally premised on that upper limit of a rise

FIG.4.1 GLOBAL ATMOSPHERIC CO_2 CONCENTRATIONS FROM 1700 TO 2021

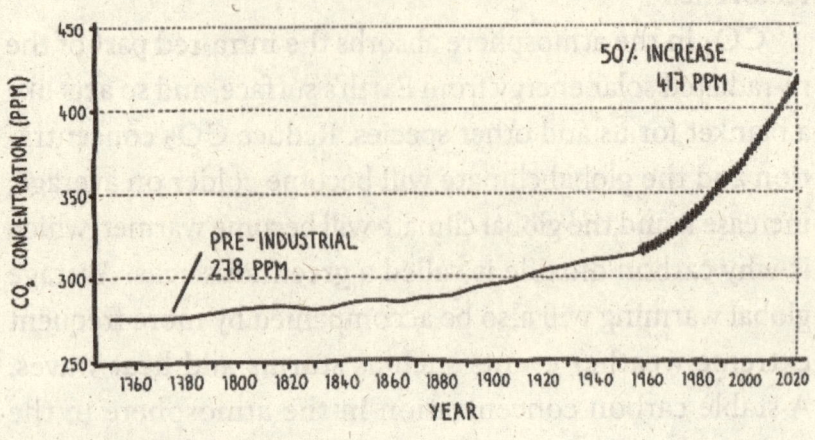

ICE CORE DATA FROM MACFARLING MEURE ET AL (2006) MAUNA LOA DATA
FROM THE SCRIPPS CO_2 PROGRAM. 2021 FORECAST FROM MET OFFICE

SOURCE: MET OFFICE

of 1.5°C, and proposals to create carbon markets were built on the idea that if people were obliged to pay to emit CO_2, they would be less inclined to emit it. A surrogate form of such a market is to require emitters to offset emissions by planting an equivalent quantity of carbon in the form of trees. But deforesting a square kilometre deep in the Amazon rainforest, thus fragmenting it, cannot simply be offset by an equivalent quantity of carbon in the form of trees planted along a motorway in the UK. Viewing climate change solely in terms of carbon emissions is to not appreciate that Nature's own climate regulation is only one of her innumerable services. It may even be that that narrowness of vision on climate is responsible for why, despite years of international negotiations, global emissions haven't declined. It is now a near-certainty that the mean temperature will rise beyond 1.5°C above pre-industrial levels, possibly by a lot more.

It is tempting to argue, however, that within the limited temperature range we have lived under, there is no sacrosanct figure for mean global temperature, and that it is the stability of the climate system that has made the past 10,000 to 12,000 years special. We should, according to this argument, be able to adjust to a warmer world with little cost, so long as the new climate system stabilises itself. But that does not recognise that our physiology and metabolism have adapted to the climate we have enjoyed over centuries. It also misses a vital feature of the assets societies throughout the world have created and accumulated. The investments we have made, not only in technologies and hardware, but also our habits and social institutions, have an irreversible element to them. Our stocks of produced and human capital for the most part cannot be transformed readily into forms that are more suitable for dramatically different climatic conditions. The need for investment in better insulated buildings or electric automobiles – and they don't come cheap – is only one example. Our hardware is more clay than putty.

We do not appreciate Nature's interwovenness in normal times, for we are accustomed to her vagaries as they fluctuate about an average. It is only when she inflicts on us a string of shocks – in the present case internally generated shocks – that we begin to appreciate the interlinkages among her processes. That appreciation continues to be absent from public discussions on ways to curb CO_2 emissions. The received economics of climate change sees a move away from fossil fuels to sources of 'clean energy', such as solar power and wind, as an escape route. But solar panels are built of silicon compounds and the blades that constitute wind farms are fibreglass-reinforced polyester. Both involve mining and quarrying, and they are two major causes of biodiversity loss.

One way to better understand the effects of climate disruption on other maintenance and regulating services, and so be better prepared, would be to ask communities across the globe about their experiences of a changing climate, the effects of those changes on their local ecosystems, and the ways both they and the ecosystems have adapted to them. It is by studying the small that we often get a glimmer of the large. Ecological economists in the Indian subcontinent and Latin America have done much valuable field work along these lines.

Commentators frequently observe that the economics of climate change can be built on one parameter, mean global temperature, which is a luxury that the economics of biodiversity does not enjoy, that is, we can try to fix climate change by just focusing on controlling the escalating global temperature, but trying to address the problems caused by a reduction in biodiversity is far more complex. That may be so, but we have seen that the correct way to view our reliance on ecosystems is to see ourselves as asset managers, and it is by studying the economics of asset management that we can best appreciate how to live within the bounds Nature sets us.

We Are All Asset Managers

Whether as farmers or fishers, foresters or miners, households or companies, governments or communities, we manage the assets to which we have access, in line with our motivations as best as we can. But the best each of us can achieve with our individual portfolios may nevertheless result in a massive collective failure to manage the global portfolio of all our assets. We are like a crowd of people, each of us trying to keep balance on a hanging bridge, only to bring it crashing down.

How would you know whether you are managing your portfolio of assets well? What rule would you follow? For simplicity, imagine there is a perfect market for every commodity: you know the price of every commodity, and the market informs you of the way the relative prices of goods and services will change over time. You have a certain amount of funds (your wealth) that you can allocate between current consumption (i.e., through spending) and saving, knowing that putting your saving into stocks, bank deposits and government bonds amounts to future consumption. So, in dividing your available wealth into current consumption and savings you are trying to create the right balance between current and future consumption. Once you do that (and it's not a trivial problem to solve, as it involves trading off your desire for consumption today against the future consumption stream you would enjoy if you added to your savings), the related next step is to determine the right investment portfolio into which you place your savings.

Let's label the dollars (or any other currency) that you have saved as W. Imagine you now want to place these W dollars in a portfolio partly made up of stocks and partly made up of a savings account in the bank. The bank offers you a fixed interest rate per year, which we label as r. You don't know exactly how much money you are going to make each year from holding the stocks, but when you adjust for your attitude to risk, the return on holding the stock is ρ. So, ρ is the 'risk-adjusted return' on holding the stock. But ρ is the sum of the stock's yield at the end of the year and the capital gains (or losses) relative to income, which together may outperform, or underperform, the savings account. In terms of your income, there wouldn't be any difference in the rate of return between holding your dollars in the bank's savings account or investing in the stocks if the two rates, ρ and r, were equal. So, if ρ and r were equal, you would be indifferent between holding your dollars in the bank and investing the dollars in the stocks. You want your portfolio of assets to be what is called 'efficient' (or 'optimal'), in that it provides the best expected return given the level of risk, or, in other words, the best risk-adjusted return. So, that's the condition the mixed portfolio must satisfy: hold only those assets that offer the maximum risk-adjusted returns. You will, at the margin, be indifferent between holding any of the assets in your efficient portfolio, because they will offer you the same (risk-adjusted) return.

Let's assume that a public agency is managing a portfolio consisting of a pair of assets. We now check whether the two assets offer the same rate of return. If we find they don't, we conclude that the agency is not managing its portfolio efficiently.

Economists have estimated that the long-run rate of return (rent or dividend) on housing and equities in the US has been round 5 per cent a year. If we choose that to be the unit of account (economists call that *numeraire*), then 5 per cent should be regarded as its yield.

Let us now contrast that with an example of yield from an item of natural capital. The economists Anil Markandya and M.N. Murty conducted a social cost–benefit analysis of an action plan of the government of India to undertake measures to raise the quality of the Ganges River water to bathing standard. The Ganges is one of the most polluted rivers in the world. The authors elicited responses to questionnaires for estimating the willingness to pay by people living in the Ganges basin for a cleaner river, and so estimated the annual social benefits to be realised by the action plan. The investment outlay and recurring costs were taken from the plan documents. Using that data, the authors estimated that the rate of return on the project to be round 15 per cent.

Consider a public agency that has shares in US housing and equities, and has an interest in how clean the Ganges is. The agency therefore can be thought to be holding both these stocks. If the portfolio was efficient, the implicit value of Ganges water should be declining relative to public income by some 10 per cent a year (the 15 per cent estimated rate of return less the 5 per cent that would be expected from investment in housing and equities).

But the evidence runs counter to that, for rapid urban

Ganges river pollution, Kolkata, India (Getty Images)

development on the Ganges basin has been worsening the quality of the river, even while income per capita in the basin has been rising. Taken together, they imply that the Ganges has become *scarcer* relative to produced capital, not more abundant (in fact, the Ganges action plan was soon abandoned, meaning that the river's water quality has been deteriorating). That is a rough and ready way of establishing the imbalance in economic development: the asset portfolio in question would be inefficient.

This familiar piece of reasoning in portfolio analysis gives us a language with which to understand what has gone so drastically wrong in our management of the biosphere. The global economy, never mind the myriads of local economies, has mismanaged the portfolio of produced capital, human capital and natural capital by *divesting* heavily from the latter in favour of the former pair, because it has *seemed* to make economic sense: natural capital doesn't obviously appear to be offering the same 'rate of return', but that consideration doesn't take into account the social value of natural capital.

Human Demand for Nature's Provisioning Goods

Society's 'ecological footprint' is the quantity of provisioning goods it draws from the biosphere in a period. What is drawn is mostly visible and recordable. It is the society's *direct* demands from Nature. The corresponding *indirect demands* – we can call them 'needs' – are for Nature's maintenance and regulating services. Humanity would be overreaching for provisioning goods if the global ecological footprint exceeded the biosphere's regeneration rate, that is, the regeneration rate of provisioning goods. We would not know of the overreach immediately, though; we would recognise it only when ecosystems begin to show signs of fatigue, requiring interventions to compensate.

If we are to identify policies that could eliminate a community's overreach, we need a way to measure it, one that is built on the community's doings. The trick is to find quantifiable measures of those doings.

Consider the global economy. We would ideally want to compare the demands it makes on each category of provisioning goods (food, water, fibres, timber and so on) and compare them to the regeneration rates of the ecosystems that supply them. It could be that the global economy over-reaches on some but not on others. In the notes to this chapter (at the end of the book), we will see how to extend the idea of ecological overreach if it is to cover individual provisioning goods, not only an aggregate of them. Here we suppose that we can aggregate our demands into a scalar measure. It is possible to do that by attaching weights to the demands we make of all categories of provisioning goods and adding them together. That would give us a combined measure of the demand humanity makes on the biosphere. The weights are known to economists as 'accounting prices'. (We discuss ways to estimate weights in Chapters 5 to 7, while accounting prices are an important feature of Chapter 8.) Below I describe an ingenious method devised by the ecologist Mathis Wackernagel and his colleagues to estimate the combined demand for provisioning goods in a period. But for now, we simply denote the combined measure of demand – the global ecological footprint – as D. In a classic paper of 1971 in *Science*, Paul Ehrlich and John Holdren read this demand (D) as being humanity's 'impact' on the biosphere.

The drivers of our ecological footprint are our activities. The common measure of humanity's activities is global GDP, which we write as Y. It is the market value of the final goods and services produced in a period (a year), expressed, say, in international dollars. But as the provisioning goods that are drawn on to produce those final goods and services do not have the dimensions of international dollars, we need a conversion factor, from dollars to the combined measure of provisioning goods that the global economy draws on to produce GDP. Let us denote GDP per unit of the combined measure of provisioning goods that are drawn upon to produce it by α. Humanity's ecological footprint is therefore GDP divided by the combined measure of provisioning goods that are drawn upon to produce it – that is, Y divided by α, or Y/α. In other words, α is the *efficiency* with which provisioning goods combine to produce GDP – the *larger* the value of α, the *smaller* the value of the combined measure of provisioning goods required to produce GDP.

We can unpick the global ecological footprint further. Global GDP is, by definition, the product of global population (N) and the global per capita GDP (y). The global ecological footprint in the period is thus global population multiplied by global per capita GDP (Ny), divided by the combined measure of provisioning goods that are drawn upon to produce GDP (i.e., α), or in other words, Ny/α. That gives us the combined global demand for provisioning goods (D). D is the global ecological footprint.

We have now identified the drivers of humanity's footprint. To put it simply, other things remaining equal, the larger the global population, the larger the footprint in that period. Similarly, the larger the per capita GDP, the larger the footprint. It is clear also that the smaller the quantity of provisioning goods that the global economy draws on to produce GDP, the smaller the footprint. In other words, the more *efficient* humanity is in converting Nature's provisioning goods into the products that add up to GDP, that is, the larger α is, the smaller the footprint.

Ehrlich and Holdren in their paper interpreted the

efficiency with which the global economy draws upon provisioning goods to produce GDP – that is, α – as an expression of the technology that is deployed to produce GDP, but institutions should also be included because they too have an influence. We will find that provisioning goods have been systematically undervalued everywhere, meaning that the global economy uses more provisioning goods to produce output than we should. And that is another way of saying that the quantity of provisioning goods that the global economy draws on to produce GDP is larger than it should be, or other words, α is *smaller* than it could be.

We now turn to the supply side. By supply, we mean Nature's net output of provisioning goods – that is, its 'yield'. As in the model of fisheries discussed in Chapter 1, we could interpret yield as the combined regeneration rate of the stock of Earth's natural capital. But to keep in line with the way we have constructed the global demand, we deploy numerical weights and create a weighted sum of the regeneration rates of ecosystems. The weights, which are numerical quantities, are needed because different ecosystems produce different sets of provisioning goods. The procedure is rather like calculating the market value of a shopping basket, in which market prices (the weights) serve to bring together, in one numerical measure of value, a variety of consumer goods. The factors that determine the regeneration rate of an ecosystem are, as in the case of the fishery, the ecosystem's size and its productivity. The weighted sum of the regeneration rates of all ecosystems would then represent a combined regeneration rate of provisioning goods, which we can call G. Below we show a way to estimate the weights.

The UN's Sustainable Development Goals

Projecting movements in our global footprint (D) and the combined regeneration rates of provisioning goods (G) over time should be at the heart of discussions on sustainable development. That has not, however, been the practice either at national levels or at the United Nations (UN). In 2015, member countries of the UN adopted a set of Sustainable Development Goals (SDGs), to be attained by 2030, as their vision for the future. They range from zero global poverty (Goal 1) to collective action among nations to bring about the Goals (Goal 17).

The intention behind producing the SDGs, 17 in number, was admirable, but the attempt reads as a desire to square the proverbial circle. For example, unless ways are found to sufficiently reduce the quantity of provisioning goods that the global economy draws on to produce GDP (that is, to raise the magnitude of α sufficiently), Goal 8 (GDP growth) would not be consistent with Goals 14–15 (to conserve and regenerate life underwater and on land). The SDGs do not unpack the constituent factors of the global ecological footprint (D). Nor did the framers of the SDGs ask whether the Goals, even if they were to be realised, would themselves be sustainable. In the event, only 4 of the 17 Goals (e.g., Goal 1, eliminating absolute poverty) are on track to be achieved.

FIG 4.2 THE UN'S SUSTAINABLE DEVELOPMENT GOALS

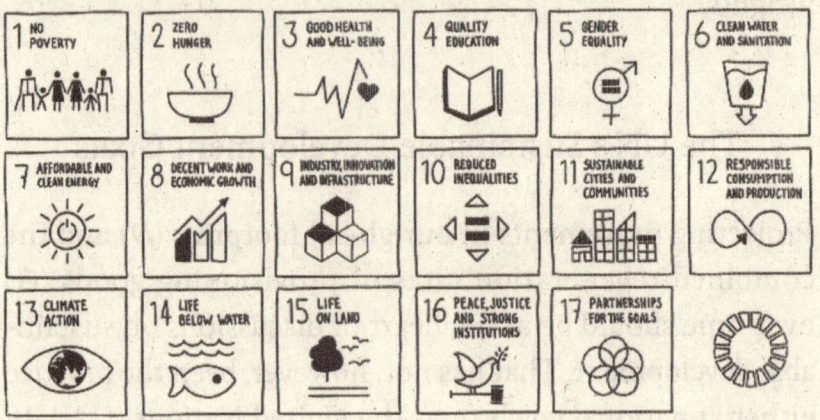

SOURCE : THE UNITED NATIONS

But the problem with the SDGs is more fundamental: they are ill suited as guides to ecological sustainability. There is a different route for developing the idea of sustainable development, which I now explore.

There is an ecological overreach in a period if global demand for the combined measure of provisioning goods exceeds Nature's combined regeneration rate. When that happens, the biosphere's productivity diminishes, which means the supply of provisioning goods is lower in the following period. To think that global demand could exceed the combined regeneration rate of provisioning goods indefinitely is to presume the biosphere to be of infinite size. Formally, there is a global ecological overreach if,

$$Ny/\alpha > G \quad (1)$$

In words, there is global ecological overreach when the global population multiplied by global per capita GDP (Ny),

96

divided by the efficiency with which provisioning goods are drawn upon to produce GDP (α), is greater than the biosphere's combined regeneration rate (G). Wackernagel and his colleagues (see below) have found that humanity's demand for provisioning goods (D) – that is, the global ecological footprint – currently exceeds the biosphere's combined regeneration rate (G). That means expression (1) – now known as the 'Impact Inequality' – holds true for the global economy.[*]

The Impact Inequality is only a snapshot of the global economy. It is an accounting statement on the state of the biosphere in a period and says nothing about the mutual interplay of global population, global per capita GDP and the quantity of provisioning goods that the global economy draws on to produce GDP, or their effect on future values of the combined regeneration rates. To study the interactions among the four variables requires a dynamic socio-ecological model.[†]

The Impact Inequality gives us a way to identify policy levers. For example, health and education policies can influence future values of global population (N), fiscal and monetary policies affect global per capita GDP (y), and institutional reforms and investment in new technologies influence the quantity of provisioning goods that the global economy draws on to produce GDP (the efficiency

---

[*] It will prove useful to remember from the Impact Inequality that, other things being equal, the larger is α, the smaller is the global ecological footprint.

[†] The *Review* contains a prototype of such a model.

parameter α). Conservation measures and what is commonly known as 'green investment' increase future values of Nature's combined regeneration rate (G). In essence, Nature's combined rate of regeneration has to play a part in any discussion of sustainable development.

Measuring Global Demand and the Combined Regeneration Rate

How might one encapsulate a combined measure of provisioning goods? One way to do that would be to follow a practice in the US, where pastures are sometimes measured in 'cow-calf' acres, which is the number of cow-calves that can be maintained on one acre. Obviously, the number of cow-calves a farm can maintain depends on the size and productivity of the pasture.

In an ingenious set of exercises, Wackernagel and his scientific collaborators deployed the same idea to estimate demand (D) and the combined regeneration rate (G) for the global economy, and for individual countries too. The authors estimated the quantity of provisioning goods humanity draws from the biosphere in a period by calculating the area of land and sea surface covering different categories of ecosystems currently deployed to produce global GDP in dollars. As against that, the authors estimated the area of land and sea surface covering different categories of ecosystems that would be needed to produce global GDP at its current level and composition on a *sustainable* basis, that is leaving space to allow for other life forms to provide pollination, seed dispersal, fertilisation, decomposition of waste, and other maintenance and regulating services that would be needed simultaneously to replenish the global stock of ecosystems. In short, the idea is to measure the land–sea area that would support current global GDP indefinitely. The authors call that Earth's 'bio-capacity'.

As examples, the land–sea area required to meet our contemporary demand for natural fibres in a period without compromising the ability of the biosphere to replenish the quantity of natural fibres that have been harvested in that period is taken to be Earth's bio-capacity for natural fibres, and the area occupied by primary producers (forests, marshes, grasslands) needed to recycle current emissions of CO_2 gases in the atmosphere is Earth's bio-capacity for carbon regulation. The same reasoning is deployed on our demands for other provisioning goods.

But ecosystems differ in their ability to provide the same service. Marshes, for example, sequester 8–10 times the carbon temperate forests do. In estimating Earth's bio-capacity for carbon recycling, Wackernagel and his colleagues for that case awarded a square kilometre of marshland a weight 8–10 as against 1 for a square kilometre of a temperate forest. They did the same for a wide range of other maintenance and regulating services. The demand the global economy makes for provisioning goods in a period is, then, a weighted sum of land–sea areas that would supply sufficient maintenance and regulating services in that same period to replenish the stocks of provisioning goods that have been depleted. This is another way to express the global demand for provisioning goods, or the global ecological footprint (D).

Against that is Nature's combined regeneration rate (G), which is estimated from the prevailing land–sea area of the world. The authors reported that global demand for provisioning goods has been increasing rapidly in recent decades, and that the ratio of global demand to the combined regeneration rate (D to G) today is about 1.7. In other words, *we need 1.7 Earths to meet humanity's current demands on a sustainable basis.*

The authors also found that global demand (D) was less than the combined regeneration rate (G) as recently as the 1960s, having crossed the equality mark in the early 1970s. We may then be tempted to think that only a few decades ago, the world economy was not overly large relative to the biosphere, maybe even that Earth was under-deployed for our purposes. But that would be a big mistake. Even though humanity lived on 'less than one Earth', and we shared it with greater numbers of other creatures, we had been closing in on them, and we paid no heed to the option value of ecosystems. We have been closing in on other life forms for a long time and are now doing so at greater speed. The figure of 1.7 for the current ratio of the global demand for provisioning goods (D) to Earth's combined regeneration rates (G) is thus an underestimate. It is most likely a serious underestimate.

As the biosphere is finite, it's supply of provisioning goods must be bounded. That means the combined regeneration rate (G) is bounded above. What then of the possibility of unending GDP growth? We could insist that, as there is no limit to human imagination, there is no limit to how any given quantity of provisioning goods can be converted into global GDP through technological and institutional improvements. So long as global GDP does not grow at a faster rate than the rate at which efficiency with which the combined measure of provisioning goods required to produce GDP (α) grows, the left-hand side of the Impact Inequality can be kept within Nature's bounds, that is, no greater than Nature's combined regeneration rate plus the slack she should be given to include the option value of ecosystems.

Thus, to take the possibility of unending GDP growth seriously would require of us to imagine that if GDP was to grow indefinitely, the *efficiency* with which the combined measure of provisioning goods required to produce GDP – that is, α – would have to grow indefinitely, and at least at the same rate as GDP, for otherwise the left-hand side of the Impact Inequality would not remain within Nature's bounds. And that requires us to imagine that no matter how gigantic the global economy becomes, investment in scientific and technological projects aiming to *further* lower the global demand for provisioning goods needed to produce a unit of GDP would become ever smaller. But that would require of us to imagine that if GDP was to become larger and larger, we would become more and more free of the biosphere. It is a view that presumes the human economy is *external* to Nature, not *embedded* in Nature. In this context our embeddedness in Nature can be read as insisting that no matter how much we invest in science and technology or improve our institutions, the quantity of provisioning goods required to produce GDP cannot be reduced beyond a certain point, which is to say that the efficiency with which provisioning goods can be converted into GDP – that is, α – cannot be increased beyond a certain point.

Ardent advocates of GDP growth have claimed that they don't foresee, nor advocate, indefinite growth, but growth only over, say, the next 100 years. For them, the long run is not an indefinite future, but a sizable future. But that explanation runs into the problem that the global economy is currently in deficit of a 1.7 ratio (maybe a lot higher) of demand to supply. Growing as much as the human economy has over the past 70 years, we have brought critical ecosystems to their near-breaking point. So, whatever 'sustainable development' could mean, it must as a minimum mean eliminating our ecological overreach.

The most urgent task facing humanity today is to find ways to bring about an equality between the global demand for Nature's provisioning goods and her ability to meet the demand on a sustainable basis. That would require lowering global demand for provisioning goods and enabling Nature to raise her combined regeneration rate. The long run is past us. We should now be concerned with now and the near future.

CHAPTER 5

The Consequences of Our Actions

What are the reasons behind humanity's large ecological overreach today? A common answer is myopia, that we don't care sufficiently for our descendants. But if someone were to ask why even 100 years ago it appeared to us that humanity hadn't overreached globally, the reply wouldn't be that people cared more about future generations than they do today, but rather that the global economy was small relative to the biosphere, and that meant there was more to be harvested and extracted at little additional stress to the biosphere. In the distant past, there was, of course, even more to be harvested and extracted.

The claim that we don't care enough about our descendants goes counter to the enormous amount of time and energy we spend on our children. The share of government expenditure on primary and secondary education in the UK, for example, is about 4.2 per cent of the country's GDP. And that doesn't include private education, nor the time and other resources parents invest in their children. One can quibble whether 4.2 per cent is adequate, but commentators complaining that it is inadequate point to the persistence of social inequalities – they don't say it is voters' myopia at work. Moreover, the answer doesn't account for why investment in produced capital, especially infrastructure, routinely has a longer lifespan than the expectancy of life of those making decisions to invest in such projects.

One might counter that even though we care about our children and take their wellbeing into account when making choices, subsequent descendants are too remote for us to care for. After all, we can do something for posterity, but what can posterity do for us? There are deep misunderstandings in this point of view (the deepest of which we expose at the very end of this book), but there is a general point: parents care about their children's wellbeing but know that their children will care about *their* children's wellbeing, and that their grandchildren in turn will care about the wellbeing of *their* children. We could thus suppose that parents take the wellbeing of their descendants into account when investing in their children. Perhaps not consciously, but selection pressure over evolutionary time will have wired us into choosing in that fashion.

But even if every household empathises with its descendants and includes their wellbeing in its own sense of wellbeing, no household would be expected to empathise in the same way with *other* households and *their* descendants. And that means no household would take account of the ecological damage its activities may cause others. In today's parlance, the situation is one where every household 'free rides' on every other household, thereby placing a greater burden on the biosphere than it would otherwise countenance.

To see what is implied by this form of free riding, imagine a chain of supermarkets with ineffective checkout counters, so ineffective that customers take home much of what they pick without paying for it. Pilfering no doubt enables people to enjoy a high living standard, but it will prove to be short-lived, for the chain in due course can be guaranteed to go bust.

Nature does not have checkout counters. We don't pay for vast quantities of the provisioning goods we rely upon, and by extension we don't pay for the maintenance and regulating services that furnish them. By 'payment', I don't necessarily mean paying a market price for a good or service, for there may not be a market for it. The payment could be the pinch we feel when facing a ration on what we are permitted to purchase in the market in times of a social emergency; or it could be the implicit price we pay when exchanging goods and services with others.

One reason we don't pay for many provisioning goods is that Nature is *mobile*. What we do at one place has consequences elsewhere, but the actions that have led to them are in many cases unpreventable, sometimes even untraceable. The phosphorus compounds that leak from farms in Midwest United States, for instance, find their way over time via the Mississippi River and its tributaries into the Gulf of Mexico, thus contributing to the enlargement of dead zones there. But the farmers don't pay for the damage they cause; their practices are more reliant on industrial fertilisers than they would be if the Gulf's ecology were part of their commercial calculations.

Unaccounted-for consequences for others of events

for which we are responsible are called *externalities*. The qualifier 'unaccounted-for' means that the consequences in question follow without prior engagement with those who are affected. As the externalities we are considering here are transmitted through the material world, we call them 'environmental externalities'.

I have provided examples of adverse environmental externalities, but environmental externalities can also be beneficial, as in the reciprocal benefits apple growers and beekeepers confer on one another. In the absence of a formal arrangement between the two groups, neither apple growers nor beekeepers would expand their activities to the extent they could with mutual benefit.

Consider also the beneficial externalities conferred on people downstream by upstream farmers when they plant trees on their land to reduce soil erosion – or the adverse externalities inflicted by farmers upstream on downstream residents if they were to further cut down trees on their land. If adverse externalities call for a reduction in the externality-generating activity, beneficial externalities call for an expansion.

But regardless of whether they are adverse or beneficial, externalities imply waste. If externalities were reduced, resources could be reallocated, making people as well-off as before, while making even fewer demands on provisioning goods. In the language of the Impact Inequality, reducing externalities, be they adverse or beneficial, lowers the quantity of provisioning goods that the global economy draws on to produce GDP – that is, it raises the efficiency with which we draw upon provisioning goods to produce GDP, namely, α. Economists say externalities harbour inefficiency in resource use, and that 'inefficiency' spells 'waste'.

Of the two types of externalities then, which is quantitatively larger in our world? The truth is, we don't know, and one reason we don't is that although societies have found ways to contain adverse externalities by instituting laws against bad behaviour, we haven't discovered ways, other than by expressing social approval, of rewarding *good* behaviour. We are not free to assault others (there are strict laws against that), but we are free not to come to the aid of others. Vast quantities of beneficial externalities remain aborted, and what is absent remains un-noted. From the societal point of view, adverse externalities need to be curbed and beneficial externalities to be encouraged. In the cases we study in this book, both contribute to an overreach in our use of resources. However, beneficial externalities accompany activities that are often hard to monitor and acknowledge. There is probably self-selection at work here; acts of charity are typically undertaken by people who deliberately keep them hidden from the prying eye – the very word 'charity' speaks to invisible acts.

The Impact Inequality could certainly be reduced if societies found ways to encourage people to engage in activities that produce beneficial environmental externalities to the point when the externalities vanish. But this remains an unexplored avenue, which is why it is useful to study the implications of adverse environmental externalities.

Open Access Resources

Under-pricing of natural capital is especially pronounced in the case of the atmosphere and the high seas. Both are non-alienable, non-excludable assets, free to all who want to make use of them, which is why they are called 'open access resources'. The adverse externalities that come allied to their use, are also reciprocal, meaning each party's activities harm all others (see below) – unaccountably, of course. Being over-arching ecosystems, the atmosphere and the high seas are what we today call global common property resources, or more commonly, 'global commons'.

In a 1954 paper that created the economics of open access resources, the economist H. Scott Gordon explained why small-scale fishermen at that time earned little income from ocean fisheries. He observed that resources (read ecosystems) that are everybody's property are nobody's property. Improvements in fishing gear, he noted, had made it profitable for many fishers to plough the seas in search of schools of fish when previously it had not been profitable. Because no one has control over how much others harvest in open access fishing grounds, no fisher can afford to care about future profits and conserve the fishery. So, Gordon argued, so long as there is income to be earned from fishing (economists call the income, net of labour and equipment costs, 'rent'), fishers will enter a fishing ground and drive down rents (which amounts to increasing the quantity of provisioning goods that the global economy draws on to produce GDP, that is, *reducing* α), until the point where there is no income to be earned. Further improvements in fishing technology would lead fishers to harvest yet more, reducing fish stocks even further. Gordon could have continued with his analysis to show that if yet further technological advances were made, an open access fishery would in due course collapse. But he didn't. That was left to later economists.

In the past 50 years, there have been several examples of the collapse of marine populations. Fish stocks have dropped precipitously in the Mediterranean Sea, making it the most overharvested fishery in the world today. The North Sea is another overfished site, where cod populations have been driven to critically low levels. In the early decades of the twentieth century the blue whale, the largest creature in the world, was nearly driven to extinction through overkill. Populations revived only because the International Whaling Commission responded by banning commercial whaling.

Fishing is but one of many activities in the high seas, including mining in the deep, pleasure cruises and the transportation of multi-billion dollars of merchandise in container ships each year. The seas are also a repository of global pollution. As no one pays rent for their use, the high seas are an open access ecosystem for those activities also. Admittedly, the harm each user inflicts on the rest of the world is negligible, but when taken collectively, the total harm isn't negligible, especially over time. In a 1968 paper in *Science*, the biologist Garrett Hardin called the overreach of open access ecosystems the 'tragedy of the commons'. He made no reference to Gordon's work, but the phrase stuck, and Hardin is widely credited with creating the economics of open access resources.

We now have an explanation for why there can be ecological overreach and the biodiversity losses that go with it even when each of us cares about the interests of our own descendants. If none of us cares sufficiently about *others'* descendants, the harm each of us inflicts on others' dynasties by overusing the global commons does not enter our calculations.

Estimating the physical extent of overreach of the global commons is possible, but placing a value on it can be contentious because judgements on how we should weigh the present relative to the future are not easy to reach. No matter how similar citizens' ethical deliberations may be, we should not expect them to reach agreement. This is confirmed in estimates of the harm carbon emissions inflict on humanity, today and over the indefinite future. Called the 'social cost of carbon', these estimates have risen over the years as more and more has been learned of the processes that translate emissions into future harm via global climate change, but there is no consensus. Some experts today place the social cost of CO_2 at 185 US dollars per ton, others demur and say it is as low as $25. And there are others who think it ought to be as high as $500.

Technological and Pricing Biases

Adverse externalities have consequences that further amplify our ecological overreach. Entrepreneurs invest in technologies that economise on costly factors of production, not cheap ones. As ecosystems are undervalued in the market-place and governments are slow to recognise their import-ance, human capital is more costly relative to natural capital than it should be. Advances in technology take the form of labour-saving devices, not Nature-saving devices. Bull-dozers, rock-breaking electric drills and chainsaws econo-mise on labour, not Nature. In the past, it would have taken many months to build a road through a tropical rainforest to extract minerals. Today it takes only weeks, involving far less brawn and sweat.

Earlier, we noted that the global demand for provision-ing goods is influenced by the technologies we use to harvest and extract them. Because natural capital is undervalued, we deploy greater quantities of provisioning goods to generate a unit of income for ourselves than we otherwise would. That spells a larger quantity of provisioning goods the global economy draws on to produce GDP (that is, a smaller α), and it boosts the left-hand side (the global demand for pro-visioning goods) in the Impact Inequality.

Ignoring adverse environmental externalities associated with commercial activities is routine practice in economics. In an influential recent book that promises superabundance on an infinitely bountiful planet, the authors explained the idea of the 'time-price' for a good or service; that is, how long it takes to earn enough to buy something. They found that the average time-price of a basket of 50 commodities, from uranium and rubber to tea and shrimp, had fallen by 72 per cent worldwide between 1980 and 2018. They saw this as technological progress at work, making resources more abundant, as new ways to find and exploit them are invented.

But the time-price of the goods in question does not include the damage done to the biosphere in the process of extraction and production (for example, shrimp farms are notorious polluters). What the authors read as unalloyed technological progress has been accompanied by an unrecorded reduction in the biosphere's provisioning goods and, concurrently, in its ability to provide maintenance and regulating services. So long as Nature's services are priced at zero in an accounting system, Earth does indeed look like being infinitely bountiful. Bad accounting practices sustain comforting myths.

A commonplace example of less-than-adequate payment for the provisioning goods people use is fast fashion, whose practice creates large, harmful externalities. Nearly a kilo of hazardous pesticides is used per hectare to produce cotton, and recycling discarded items of clothing, following on average eight uses, is a small fraction of total sales. If it costs a certain number of dollars in an otherwise competitive marketplace to produce an item of fast fashion but inflicts another amount of dollars of unaccounted for harm when producing, using and discarding it, the real cost of production of the item is not the production cost but the production cost *plus the cost of the harm*, and that implies the item's sales price should be no less than the two costs combined.

Not to include the cost of the harm in the price of the fashion item means that the combined measure of provisioning goods indicated in the price is smaller than it really is. In writing about the fast fashion industry, the author Dana Thomas has come close to suggesting that the cost of harm is so large that if it was included in the price people must pay, the industry would be a shadow of what it is today.

So, the questions are: on what basis should the price of provisioning goods be estimated? How should the harm caused by externalities (the cost of the harm in the previous example) be calculated? Who is to collect the payments? What governance structures are likely to be most effective in eliminating environmental externalities?

The Public Viewpoint and Personal Wellbeing

When we ask these questions, we know at once we are viewing the world with a wider lens than we do when shopping in the supermarket. We adopt what may be called the 'public viewpoint'. We do not want to choose what to do and act on the basis solely of our personal wellbeing, a reflection of our 'inner-directed viewpoint', but want to include the wellbeing of others too. We do not know most of those others, of course, but they are not impossible to understand. We recognise that, as we were all drawn from the same evolutionary pool, there is a commonality among us humans, and that we all have a common set of needs to make life go well and a common set of requirements for those needs to be met. In the public viewpoint, we empathise with others. Which is why we aren't reluctant to compare our own wellbeing with the wellbeing of people experiencing different circumstances and facing different life prospects from our own.

The lens we deploy for assuming the public viewpoint depends on the issue in hand. Over global matters that have irreversible consequences, such as our use of the atmosphere as a sink for carbon emissions, the lens would be widest. We realise that the burden of global climate change is likely to be borne by some of the world's poorest people, and that if our activities risk tipping the climate system into a new, wholly unfamiliar regime, the cost will be borne mostly by future people. The public we would include in our thinking is the global population and their descendants.

Over regional environmental matters, such as sharing a river estuary, the lens would be less wide, but the public in question would include people and their families beyond our own border. The lens would narrow down to people in our own country if we were trying to form a view of, say, the environmental regulations our national government ought to put in place to keep our wetlands from disappearing altogether.

The lens would be perhaps the narrowest when the concern is over our own neighbourhood. We want to lobby our local council to permit us to create a green space on land that could be used to build a couple of new homes. We weigh the two options in our mind and cast our eye over the affected population, our neighbours at large. Such an issue could appear negligible in the big scheme of things, but it matters to us and is something on which we have some say as well as control. There is also the comforting thought that it is when we consider the very small that we as individuals are most able to protect and promote biodiversity. The tropical rainforests are foreign to us – they are an ecosystem that has been shaped in our minds from reading articles and watching documentaries; they are an *intellectual* concern. Our local ecosystem is a different matter. We are aware of its presence viscerally and care about its state deeply. Working with neighbours to create a small Nature reserve amidst a concrete landscape gives us pleasure, gives us something enriching to do, and is ultimately satisfying.

The public viewpoint enables us to identify 'public morality', the morality that guides those of our actions that have an impact on others. There is an enormous amount of literature on the subject. For our purposes, though, we shall adopt a narrower conception, and think of public morality as being built on the personal wellbeing of all who come in sight under our lens.

An individual's 'personal wellbeing' – some call it 'happiness' – is gleaned from an 'inner-directed viewpoint'. It is the extent to which a person's informed desires are realised, and that 'extent' can be represented numerically.* As desires, whether informed or not, are an expression of preferences over alternatives, the raw materials for building the notion of personal wellbeing are 'informed preferences'. We are not talking of mere gratification of desires here, for the qualifier 'informed' is meant to bear ethical weight. The fulfilment of informed desires characterises a flourishing life. Moreover, we are to think of a *whole life* (as in 'life satisfaction'), not

---

* This idea is developed further in Chapter 6.

just a slice of it (the latter could simply reflect a mood), from every aspect and all the way down. And it includes not only a person's engagement with herself and with other people, but also a recognition by her that she is embedded in Nature. Going through life oblivious of Nature is a blunted life.

Personal ethics, involving an inner-directed viewpoint, are the first tier of ethical reasoning. Public morality, the space in which the public viewpoint is adopted, is the second. What we seek to uncover when we adopt the public viewpoint is the wellbeing of a body collective, or what we can call 'social wellbeing'. Policies that are likely to enhance social wellbeing are socially good. Depending on the context, social wellbeing could be the collective wellbeing of the global population at one end, or it could be, at the other end, the collective wellbeing of people in our immediate neighbourhood.

When we adopt the public viewpoint, it is necessary that we compare the wellbeing of different people. We therefore need, first, a way to measure personal wellbeing. We could do that by obtaining a person's informed preferences over alternatives and then seek information about her intensity of preferences; that is, noting not only that she prefers alternative A to alternative B, and alternative B to alternative C, but also that her preference for A over B is so many times her preference for B over C. We also compare the personal wellbeing of different people as, for example, when we say, 'Sue is in a much better place than Bill.' The judgement requires that personal wellbeing is measurable and that interpersonal comparisons of wellbeing are possible. That may seem a tall order, but implicitly we do it all the time.

In practical reasoning, it has proved fruitful to draw on Utilitarianism, in which social wellbeing is judged to be a weighted sum of individual wellbeings, the weights reflecting the trade-offs among different people's wellbeing that we think are permissible when we deliberate over alternative economic paths. For evaluating policies that have long-term consequences, the public viewpoint includes future generations. In that case, a pragmatic formulation of Utilitarian calculus would prescribe that we use a weighted sum of individual wellbeings, where the weights reflect the trade-offs that the person assuming the public viewpoint accepts as reasonable, all things considered, between people today and people of future times. To the pragmatist among us, those weights are not given by *a priori* reasoning but are instead arrived at only after the person has studied their implications – for human wellbeing and Nature – in an iterative process involving thought-experiments.*

To see how this works, remember that in choosing between policies – say, between alternative rates of environmental taxes and subsidies – we are choosing between possible futures. So, we need quantitative models characterising possible futures and we need a conception of social wellbeing. We then choose the best from those possible futures open to us and see whether the choice seems right.

---

* Classical Utilitarian thinking would have it otherwise. It would instead posit that the weights decline with the temporal distance individuals have from us; that is, the needs/wants of people in the far future have less weight than those of present and next generations. According to this viewpoint the declining weights do not reflect myopia, but rather a way the prescriber incorporates future uncertainty into her reasoning.

If the choice doesn't seem right (perhaps it does not even pass the smell test), we revise the parameters of our formulation of social wellbeing and look again for the best possible future from it. The process is iterative, for at the end of the day if our conception of social wellbeing doesn't direct us to economic futures that look right – for example, good or just – we should not accept them but try harder to find what, in a deep intuitive sense, feels right.

A long-standing philosophical tradition, dating back to the ancients, has it that social good is an absolute, that it can be discerned as a Platonic truth of unwavering exactitude, if only we try hard enough to identify it. Translated into the vocabulary we are adopting here, the tradition has it that no two people adopting the public viewpoint could disagree over which public policies to support once they had given matters sufficient empathetic consideration and shared the same information about the possible futures. The philosopher Thomas Nagel has called this perspective of the social good 'the view from nowhere'.

The tradition should be resisted. There is a subjective element each of us brings to public morality. We humans may share the commonality of being human, but we are each a distinct organism, and all have unique perspectives. Even if two concerned citizens shared the same underlying philosophy to guide their thinking, they would not be expected to reach complete agreement on what the best set of environmental policies is, and their construction of social wellbeing would not necessarily be the same, for if nothing else, it may be that their comparisons of personal wellbeing among people differ. Concerned citizens live in a world where people can agree to disagree. In democratic societies, their disagreements are resolved at the ballot box under a fair voting rule. People would be expected to disagree over what is a fair voting rule. So, they would use political persuasion, as they do in democratic societies, to modify voting rules when the occasion arises.

CHAPTER 6

The Influence of Others

Externalities are not limited to the material environment; they also appear in the mental world. Such externalities appear in those spheres of life where we are socially embedded. We are not pure egoists in all things; we care about what others say and do, and what others think of us, and this affects our personal wellbeing. Moreover, we know what we say and do influences others. In the distant past, those others were our kinship; subsequently, in urban life, perhaps our neighbours. We sometimes call them our peers. Today, the sphere of influence is a lot more extensive than previously, as television, the internet and social media have widened our 'peer group'. It is significant that the psychological pressures to act one way or another are internal to us. We are not necessarily bullied into doing what we do – the choice is often voluntary. In contrast, the psychological pressures we experience from social norms arise from external sources, even if only tacitly.

The most obvious influence of others on our current self is our own past choices. Of course, our past choices were themselves influenced by what others then said or did (inevitably, our family was a strong influence in our earliest years), but the channel through which those choices have influenced our current selves is our past selves. The accumulation of those choices and their consequences are called 'experience', and we recognise that even our aspirations are influenced by our experiences. Nevertheless, they would not necessarily give rise to externalities. If a person had anticipated, even if hazily, the effect of what she chose to do on her subsequent wellbeing, she would have adjusted her choices to take that into account. We may be different selves as we move through time, but those selves are connected in a way that our composite self is not connected with other selves.

Socially Embedded Preferences

The fact that consumption is an activity around which human relationships are built and maintained has been expressed time and again by classicists, historians and anthropologists in their studies of traditional societies. Feasts to mark occasions of significance (birth, puberty, marriage, death, harvests and the annual renewal that is spring) are a recurrent theme in writings by the ancients. The epic poems of both the Greek poet Homer and the Hindu sage Vyasa are filled with them. There is hardly a book in the *Odyssey* that does not have a line-by-line description of the roasting, carving and communal eating of meat and drinking of wine. And no opportunity is lost in the *Mahabharata* for describing the extravagance with which kings entertain their kinsmen and guests to mark a sacrifice to the gods or to celebrate the establishment of a capital for their kingdom.

By consumption, I don't only mean food. The ancients were eager to point to the fineries enjoyed by aristocrats. A king's greatness was displayed by royal robes, the size of their retinue and the magnificence of their palace. But it is food that the ancient bards return to time and time again. Historians of consumption are aware that the act of eating food communally has been a salient feature of societies everywhere, and that feasts have bound societies together since time immemorial. What contemporary historians have sought to understand are the societal changes that led to the democratisation of eating meals together, for the feasts described in epic poetry are enjoyed only by the aristocrats, and we are told little of how common people celebrated special occasions. The modern historian, in contrast, may wish to understand the growth of inns, cafés and restaurants in the general development of societies in the West since the Late Middle Ages and Early Modern times.

Reproduction, however, could appear to the modern mind as a deeply private aspect of our lives, but in many contemporary societies the status of women is related to her fertility. That there is a preference for sons in many places has been much documented; national policies to restrict the number of births per household have been known to be followed by markedly skewed ratios between the genders. The ancients, as always, were sensitive to cultural impera-tives. Homer tells us that King Priam of Troy had 50 sons; Vyasa speaks of the hundred sons of King Dhritarashtra of Hastinapura. It would seem sons gave status to a king – the more in number, the higher the status attained.

The externalities that these 'socially embedded

preferences' create differ from environmental externalities in a crucial respect. If informed preferences are the basis on which public policies are designed, there is no reason they should be designed to exclude the influence of others. On the contrary, to imagine that there is a reason would be to favour a busy-body government, or worse, Big Brother. Externalities traceable to socially embedded preferences arise not because others' choices influence our preferences, but because the choices are made by *them*, not us. It could be that we are competitive with others in one field of activity but want to conform with others in another. In the former case, we would enter a rat race; in the latter, we would behave like the others. In either case, it could be that we would all prefer to act differently, but do not find it in our individual interests to do so. Each of these cases harbours consumption externalities – because they drive consumption – and places further pressure on Nature's provisioning goods.

If our preferences for consumption goods are socially embedded, it must be that our income relative to that of others matters to us. Analyses of data collated from responses to questionnaires on how satisfied people are with their lives (the Eurobarometer surveys are a key source today) have found that rich people express greater life satisfaction than poor people in society, but that over time people do not express greater life satisfaction when their incomes rise proportionately (so in the long term, growth rates of happiness and income are not closely related). The finding, noted first by the economist Richard Easterlin in the 1970s, is known as the Easterlin Paradox, but the fact that our preferences include comparing ourselves to others tells us that this should not be seen as a paradox at all. (Nor did Easterlin say his finding was paradoxical; he instead concluded that relative income matters to us.)

Development economists have paid little attention to the role played by socially embedded preferences in reproductive choice. Not so with demographers, who have explored the influence of a society's culture on its fertility outcomes. However, the questionnaires they have designed to elicit women's desired family size preclude the idea that women's desired family size may be an expression of their socially embedded preferences. If they had been designed to acknowledge socially embedded preferences, cultural differences would have been found to have less power to explain differences in fertility outcomes. We confirm that presently.

Socially embedded preferences, whether they are over-consumption or family size, are not routine fares in economics. You will not find many statistical studies estimating the contribution others' consumption or reproductive choices make on one's own choices. That is why we shall rely on the writings of anthropologists, sociologists and historians, which, however, offer mostly qualitative evidence. For reasons that will become clear, we will study socially embedded preferences with examples of consumption practices in high-income countries and reproductive behaviour in low-income countries. The analysis points to patterns of behavioural change that would lower our impact on the biosphere – our ecological footprint – by reducing future values of global per capita GDP (y) and global population (N), respectively, in the Impact Inequality.

Consumption Preferences

There are two broad categories of socially embedded preferences for consumption: 'competitive' and 'conformist'. The
phenomenon of conspicuous consumption, studied by the
sociologist Thorstein Veblen in the late nineteenth century,
was interpreted by him in terms of competitive preferences.
Veblen wrote about the motivations of the super-rich in the
Gilded Age of the late nineteenth-century USA that drove
them to build ever more dazzling private mansions. He read
them as a desire for high social status, hence 'status goods'.
Competitive preferences for a category of goods give rise to
a pressure to be profligate in their purchase, something we
often acknowledge ourselves. They skew our expenditure
patterns and are ultimately self-defeating because others
are also under pressure to spend more. What keeps us from
going over the top is limited budget. Of course, if we had
competitive preferences of equal strength over *all* categories
of consumption goods, there would be fewer biases in our
consumption pattern, they would cancel out, and our pur-
chases would be as though our preferences were not competitive after all. But the anguish in having to tend to each of our
competitive urges would probably cause us to lose our sanity.

Competitive preferences are what lie behind the term
'consumerism', which carries with it a pejorative note.
Studies suggest people acknowledge the force of the rat races
they join in search of consumption experiences and recognise that they all would be better off not joining the rush
to consume. But they also acknowledge they don't have an

incentive to unilaterally withdraw from the competition.* Taxes on conspicuous consumption are a way to dampen our enthusiasm for it. Environmental and behavioural externalities arising from competitive consumption, taken together, create substantial pressure on the biosphere's provisioning goods.

Conformist preferences, in contrast, embody a desire to be *like* others, to belong, to not stand out, to make choices close to those made by others. Fads and fashions in the choice of food, clothing, home appliances, reading and entertainment are among the most striking examples. But there are subtler expressions. When we invite friends to dinner, we follow rituals that avoid any risk of being seen to be showing off. If we serve wine of a higher-than-expected quality, we probably do so to show appreciation of our friendship and are quick to say as much; most of us are keen not to display wealth. The late, great social anthropologist, Mary Douglas, once remarked that poverty is when you are ashamed to invite your neighbour home to tea.

Conformist preferences give rise to processes resembling the spread of infectious diseases. Imagine a group of trendsetters or celebrities. Today, they are frequently employed by corporations to advertise products. Say, a celebrity claims she uses a new brand of a trainer. Those who are her avid fans switch to the brand even though they incur a cost in doing so. The proportion of people who now use the brand increases, and a group not necessarily in awe of the celebrity

---

* Game theory has provided a general formulation of such 'arms races' via the well-known 'Prisoners' Dilemma' game.

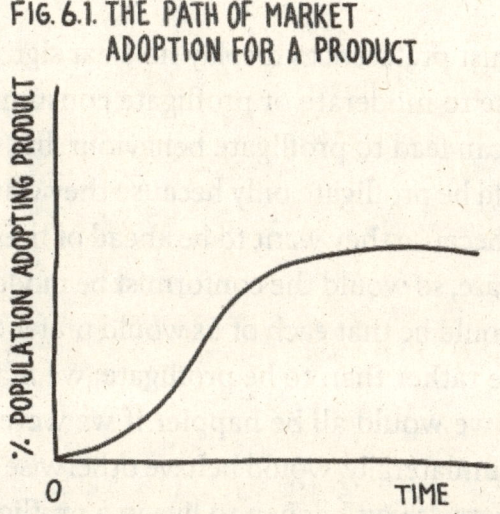

FIG. 6.1. THE PATH OF MARKET
ADOPTION FOR A PRODUCT

switch brands because they know people in the group who have done so. That induces further people to switch brands, and so on. The urge is contagious. Fig. 6.1 displays the spread of contagion in a population. Of course, the corporation may not be able to take over the entire market, which it shares with rivals advertising their own products with the help of other celebrities. The point remains, though, that product niches get established through contagion.

It is not always easy to tell from a person's choices whether her preferences are socially embedded or whether she is an egoist but whose choices are based on information other people's behaviour conveys to her. Imagine someone joining a queue at a cinema. She could be an egoist joining the queue because the queue suggests to her the film must be good, but it could be that she wants others to know she has watched the film. But there are examples that are not ambiguous. Flared trousers became the rage among men in the UK in the 1970s, but then disappeared for no apparent reason.

Conformist preferences display no clear sign of whether they give rise to moderate or profligate consumption practices. They can lead to profligate behaviour, but conformist people would be profligate only because they want to be *like* others, not because they want to be ahead of them. If others were moderate, so would the conformist be moderate. Interestingly, it could be that each of us would prefer everyone to be moderate rather than to be profligate; we may even recognise that we would all be happier if we were moderate, but no one, unilaterally, would behave otherwise if all others were profligate. If you happen to live in a profligate society, you, a conformist, would be profligate. Which social equilibrium ('moderate' or 'profligate') you would find yourself in could depend entirely on a sequence of historical accidents. As the example of the influence of celebrities showed, it could have been a different celebrity, displaying a different brand that depends on far fewer provisioning goods, that began the imitation process.

Conformist preferences give rise to a range of policy options. Because people want to be close to one another in their consumption choice, public appeals via publicity campaigns could be a way to coordinate individual consumption to collectively desired levels. But the effectiveness of such appeals depends on whether actions are observable. On policies to mitigate against climate change, it has been found to be easier to encourage people to purchase electric cars than it is to persuade people to decarbonise the heating systems in their homes.

However, information that people are changing their behaviour can have an effect. A study in the US found that when cafeteria diners were told that an increasing proportion of people were reducing their meat intake, they were twice as likely to order a meat-free option. Then, there are subtler methods of persuasion. Nudging people to make them choose one way rather than another is an example (see Chapter 9).

Our consumption behaviour over some categories of goods and services has been found to be competitive, in others it has been found to be conformist, in still others it resembles that of the egoist who ignores the crowd.

Goods and activities conferring status (cosmetics, high-end tourism, fashion and leather goods) are frequently built on primary products from tropical, biodiverse countries; and while demand for them increases the material standard of living, it simultaneously widens the Impact Inequality. However, which goods and activities are awarded status is, as we have noted, in part a matter of accidents of choice. If, in view of the Impact Inequality, we were able to coordinate among ourselves and award status to goods and activities that make less demands on Nature, perhaps even those that enhance her, it would be a route to sustainable development. Our urge to conform would reinforce that change in direction.

The key point remains; neither our competitive urge nor our conformist leanings are the source of our ecological overreach. What has been our fault is not to acknowledge that we must act collectively if we are to curb our demands; simultaneously we have chosen resource-intensive goods and activities to serve as the gold standard of living well. Paradoxical though it may seem, it is our socially embedded preferences that could come to our rescue and guide us away from such choices, but only if we recognise they can.

Demographic Choices

The global population today is over 8.1 billion. That is more than three times the global population in 1950. Declines in mortality rates have not been matched by declines in fertility rates in this period. But population trends have differed greatly across regions. Fig. 6.2, taken from the 2024 publication of the UN Population Division (UNPD) on global population trends in eight regions covering the world, shows that population has grown in every region since 1950.

FIG 6.2 UNPD WPP 2024 POPULATION ESTIMATES AND PROJECTIONS 1950-2100

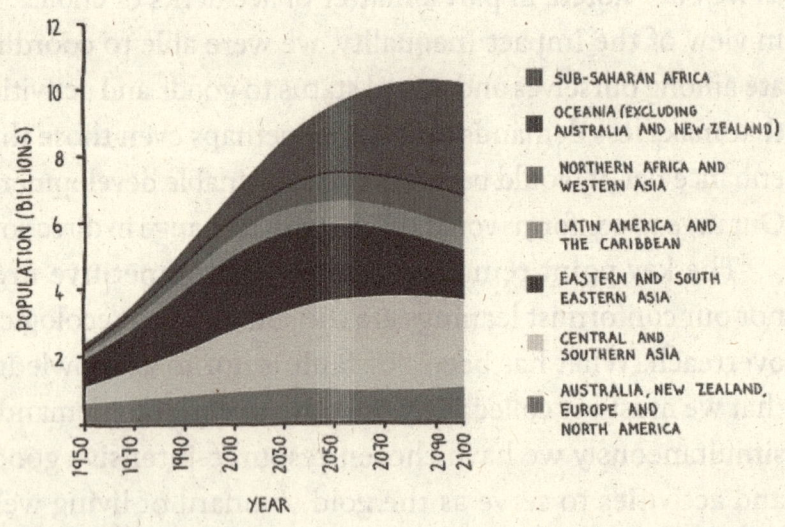

SOURCE: UNPD (2024)

Table 6.1, based on Fig. 6.2, presents estimates of changes in population numbers between 1950 and 2023 in five regions of the world: Europe, (East, Southeast and South) Asia, (sub-Saharan) Africa, North America and South America. It shows that differences in reproductive outcomes, past and present, are sharpest in Asia and Africa. Asia's population grew by 3.4 billion, from 1.4 billion to 4.8 billion. It was 56 per cent of the global population in 1950; today it is around 59 per cent. In contrast, Africa's population grew from 180 million to approximately 1.2 billion. In 1950 it was a mere 7 per cent of the global population and is even today under 14 per cent.

TABLE 6.1: POPULATION NUMBERS AND TOTAL FERTILITY RATES 1950–2023

	Population (millions)		Total fertility rates (TFR)	
	1950	2023	1950	2023
(E, SE & S) Asia	1,400	4,800	6.1	1.9
Europe	550	742	2.7	1.5
(Sub-Saharan) Africa	180	1,200	6.5	4.5
North America	166	380	3.4	1.7
South America	165	440	5.8	1.8
World	2,500	8,100		

Source: UNPD (various years). NB: several regions are absent from the table.

The gold standard for measuring reproductive behaviour in a society is its total fertility rate (TFR). TFR is the number of times on average a woman gives birth over her reproductive years, taken to be 15–49. Correcting for early mortality, 2.1 has been found to be a good approximation of a TFR at which population, in time, would be constant, which is why 2.1 is regarded as the replacement (fertility) rate.

But reproductive behaviour does change in every society, so, this year's TFR is not necessarily last year's TFR and cannot tell us next year's TFR. By tracking past movements, however, demographers can estimate changes in the age composition of a population to the present. Using a society's past trends in those variables, they can also use standard statistical techniques to make projections of future TFRs, and thus future population numbers and their age compositions. There is inevitably a subjective element in any such exercise, as past behaviour and outcomes may not be a reliable guide to future behaviour and outcomes.

Even though TFRs in Asia and Africa were similarly high in 1950 (6.1 and 6.5, respectively), Asia has made a fertility transition since then to 1.9. (The TFR in India today is around 2.1; in China it is a low 1.0.) In contrast, Africa's remains high at 4.7. That says something about differences in the regions' socio-economic experiences in recent decades and could prove to be a harbinger of further differences over the coming years.

South America, a predominantly Catholic region, made a fertility transition from a TFR of 5.8 to 1.8, suggesting that religion may have little to do with the likelihood of a fertility transition in the modern world. Every region barring

Africa has made a transition from above the replacement rate to below it, which further suggests that what are loosely regarded as 'cultural differences' are not rigid, at least not as they express themselves in fertility rates. But high TFRs in the recent past mean large proportions of young people in society today. So, even after a region makes the transition to a TFR less than the replacement rate of 2.1, it takes time for the population to reach a peak and begin a decline. A population's 'momentum' leaves an imprint of the past on the present and future. Taken together, Fig. 6.2 and Table 6.1 display this.

What of the future population? Fig. 6.2 shows that the global population in the year 2100 is projected to be 10.4 billion. That's the *median* projection, the middle value of the estimates. With the exception sub-Saharan Africa, Oceania (excluding Australia and New Zealand) and North Africa and West Asia, population in the rest of world when taken together is projected to stabilise in a few years. Central, South and East and Southeast Asia's population is projected to decline from the current 4.4 billion to 4.2 billion by 2100.

In sharp contrast, sub-Saharan Africa's population is projected to rise from roughly 1.1 today billion to 3.4 billion in 2100, a nearly three-fold increase in approximately 75 years. But that's the median projection. If we include uncertainty intervals, the total population could be somewhere between 2.8 billion and 4.3 billion with 80 per cent certainty. The actions taken now will influence whether total population will be at the lower or upper end of the probabilistic projections.

What if we redo the population projections by studying

the uncertainty bands in the UN Population Division's formulation? The 80 per cent lower bound on global population for 2100 is 9.3 billion. Judging by that figure, we should be considering a planet inhabited by at least 1 billion more people at the end of the century. We do not have any quantitative estimates of the environmental implications of 9.3 billion people enjoying what would be hoped to be a higher standard of living (y) than now. There is an urgent need to study the couplings among population growth, livings standards and the dynamics of the biosphere.

There is a common belief that because global population *growth* is slowing down (Fig. 6.2), population numbers are not a problem. This belief is reinforced by the macroeconomic models in use even by international organisations such as the World Bank and the UN Development Programme (UNDP), which are mandated to think about the long run. The problem with their models is that they don't ask whether the biosphere could sustain 9.3 billion people enjoying what, presumably, would be hoped to be a higher standard of living than today's approximately 19,000 international dollars a year. The implicit assumption is that it can. The institutions have avoided asking the question by simply keeping Nature out of their macroeconomic models.

The belief is in any case based on defective reasoning. So long as population growth is positive, global population increases in the Impact Inequality even if the growth rate is projected to decline. And the Impact Inequality reminds us that, in any period, Nature responds to the *demand* we make for her provisioning goods; she does not recognise the rate of change of demand. Growth in the global population size, so long as it is positive, will make further demands on provisioning goods, other things being equal, reducing further Nature's supplies of maintenance and regulating services from what they are currently.

The Impact Inequality is a snapshot of the gap between our demand for provisioning goods and the biosphere's regeneration rate; it doesn't say how the factors affecting our demand influence one another over time, nor does it project their future movements. If we want the inequality gap to close, something will have to give, but to date there has been no discussion in official circles of what that would be. Instead, leaders of wealthy countries and emerging economies worry that with TFRs below replacement rate, there will be a dearth of workers in their countries to fuel GDP growth.

Reproductive Choices

Regions that are commonly thought to have different cultures have made the fertility transition to below 2.1 from different starting points in only a few decades. This has been attributed to factors such as improvements in property relationships within and among households; and the rise in women's education and their higher participation in the formal labour market, improved access to family planning and reproductive health services, and a rise in their age of marriage.

As the latter measures reflect increases in women's empowerment, the term is now much used in discussions on the prospects of fertility transitions in Africa, the one continent where the TFR remains well above replacement rate. The idea is that even if household reproductive preferences differ across regions, improvements in the terms at which women can negotiate their lives would translate into a common reproductive goal: smaller family size. The rapid fertility transition in Taiwan from a high of 4 in 1970 to the replacement rate of 2.1 in 1984 – a mere 15 years – is an example of how cultural practices can change rapidly in a society previously regarded as traditional.

Women's empowerment is a fundamental social good, period; it doesn't require defence. But for policy analysis, demographers need to estimate the influence of women's empowerment on fertility outcome. The problem, however, is that factors contributing to empowerment are very likely not independent of one another; for example, it could be that the age at which women marry is related to their access to the formal labour market, or to education. If the explanatory factors are related to one another positively, we know they are all desirable, but it doesn't tell the policy maker how to allocate resources among them. A further problem is that the resources available to a government to empower women may be so limited that there is little choice to explore among alternative expenditures. This is especially true in Africa, where the average income is less than a quarter of the global average, which is why it pays to explore further avenues for societal engagement there.

One way to translate the influence of cultural imperatives on reproductive choices is to ask women for their desired family size. Demographers do that by asking women a variety of questions, one of which relates to the family size they desire, as in 'if you could go back to the time when you did not have any children and could choose exactly the number of children to have in your whole life, how many would that be?' The desired number of children in Asia has been found to be around 1.7, whereas in Africa it is 4.5, which is taken to explain differences in fertility rates (TFRs) in the two regions.

However, this method does not acknowledge that fertility preferences can be socially embedded. Reproductive behaviour is conformist when the family size a household desires stays close to the average family size in the community or, more broadly, in the world the household encounters, via magazines, billboards, television and now the internet. As with conformist consumption practices, conformist fertility preferences can be associated with multiple possible outcomes. It could be that so long as all others aim at large families, no household will wish to deviate from the practice, but that if all other households were to restrict their family size, every household would wish to restrict its family size. A society can thus get embedded in a self-sustaining mode of behaviour characterised by high fertility and stagnant living standards, even when there is another potentially self-sustaining mode of behaviour characterised by low fertility and rising living standards and that is preferred by all. Large differences in fertility behaviour across societies could suggest differences in cultures, but it might not be that at all. It may be that the people in all the societies in question are influenced by their respective peer group but behave differently only because their peer group in each society chooses differently.

Regrettably, a woman is not asked what her desired family size would be if the prevailing reproductive practices of others in her peer group were different. In fact, there is no mention even of the prevailing TFR. A direct way to discover socially embedded preferences would be to reconstruct the questionnaire by asking a series of conditional questions, which may be collapsed here into one: 'If you could go back to the time when you did not have any children and could choose exactly the number of children to have in your whole life, how many would that be, assuming everyone else in your community had *n* children over their whole life?' The thought I am exploring here is that it may be that Asian and African women have similar preferences but are expressing different fertility desires because their societies are in different social equilibria.

That conformist preferences can support multiple social equilibria tells us also that we may be mistaken in seeking causal connections between variables when there may be none. A famous study using data on TFRs and desired fertility rates from 43 countries in Asia, Africa and Latin America found that about 90 per cent of cross-country differences in TFR were associated with differences in desired fertility rates, and that excess fertility (TFR minus desired fertility rate) was not systematically related to actual TFR, nor an important determinant of it. The study concluded that in a region where TFR is high, it is high because of a strong desire for children.

If the inference were correct, it would be an important finding, for it would say that fertility rates differ across societies because fertility *desires* differ. But the inference is not correct. If people choose in line with their socially embedded preferences, it would be no truer to say fertility rates where the TFRs are high are high because people have a strong desire for children than it would be to say that people have a strong desire to have children because fertility rates are high.

Not many demographic studies have been built on socially embedded reproductive preferences, but a few stand out. A study of contraceptive use in rural Kenya found that in communities where there are dense social networks and a poorly developed market economy, a woman would be unlikely to use contraceptive methods if contraception use in her network was low, whereas she would be likely to use such methods if contraception use in her network was high. That reproductive behaviour is guided by attention to others was also found in an analysis of a natural experiment, which found that state-level fertility rates declined in step following staggered introductions of cable TV across Indian states in the 1980s.

But perhaps the most convincing evidence of socially embedded reproductive preferences has come from a famous experiment initiated in 1977 by the International Centre for Diarrheal Disease Research in Dhaka, Bangladesh, with technical support from Population Council in New York, to test the benefits of family planning and reproductive health programmes. A control area was chosen in Matlab, a *thana* (or sub-district) in Bangladesh, where people received the same limited family-planning and reproductive-health services as the rest of the country. A separate experimental area in Matlab was then provided with free services and supplies, home visits by trained female family-planning workers, and a comprehensive media communication outreach to husbands and village and religious leaders to address potential familial and social objections.

Use of contraceptives jumped from 5 per cent to 33 per cent among married women of reproductive age in the experimental area. A difference of about 1.5 births per woman between the experimental and control areas was observed by 1990, and a smaller difference continued until 1996 when the experiment ended. Among the long-term consequences of this difference in fertility rates are better educated children in the experimental area, larger household assets, greater use of preventive health services, greater birth-spacing (the gap between having children) and lower child mortality. Subsequent studies have found that the decline in the TFR continued beyond 1996 and, as would be expected from con-formist behaviour, spread elsewhere. Bangladesh's TFR in 1977 was 6.6; today it is 1.9.

Africa's Exceptionalism

Per capita GDP in (sub-Saharan) Africa is less than 20 per cent of the global GDP per capita; the region's GDP is 2–3 per cent of global GDP. That latter figure means Africa is not remotely responsible for today's *global* ecological overreach. But the region's demands on its *own* ecosystems exceed their ability to meet the demands on a sustainable basis; direct evidence for which is its many deteriorating ecosystems. IPBES has estimated that some 20 per cent of land surfaces in the subcontinent falls in the category of degraded land. It also suggests that by 2100 more than half of the region's bird and mammal species could well be lost, and the productivity of the subcontinent's lakes could decline by 20–30 per cent. The subcontinent suffers from a regional version of the Impact Inequality; demand for the provisioning goods supplied by Africa's ecosystems exceeds their regeneration rates, the ratio of the two being 1.2: 1.5. Which is why high fertility rates in the region can be expected to dampen the prospects of future Africans enjoying flourishing lives.

All governments today acknowledge the importance of investment in women's education. Unfortunately, that it is a ready road to women's empowerment in the world's poorest countries is not borne by evidence, for education involves more than school buildings. Teaching materials need to be provided and teachers themselves should be qualified. There must also be a guarantee that teachers take their classes, and that children attend them and are in a fit state of health to be able to concentrate and learn. Achieving each requires citizens' insistence that each of the factors is attended to. There is evidence that the combination has proved hard to achieve in the world's poorest countries. Even today, more than 25 per cent of women between 15 and 24 years of age in Africa are illiterate. Moreover, what qualifies as literacy is woefully inadequate for the modern world.

The UN's SDGs were fashioned seemingly with little attention to either demography or the possible difficulties low-income countries face in using investment in education as a springboard for women's empowerment. A 2013 study from UNESCO estimates that to meet the SDG target of universal primary schooling by 2030, the number of teachers

will have to increase by 2.1 million; and to achieve universal lower secondary schooling by 2030 in Africa will require
an expansion of the number of teachers from 1 million to
3.5 million. That estimate was made some years ago, so the
numbers have risen. The percentage of trained teachers in
primary education is round two-thirds and in secondary
education it is 50 percent. Today nearly 20 per cent of 11 to
12 year-olds are illiterate and 30 per cent are innumerate in
a sample of 14 countries in Africa.

What does our account of socially embedded reproductive preferences tell us about Africa's high fertility rates? It
tells us to be wary of suggestions that they reflect a culture so
ingrained that to speak on the subject is to show disrespect
to Africans. And it tells us not to attribute fertility behaviour
to women's desired fertility rates obtained from questionnaires in the form they have been framed. What is relatively
easy to achieve even in low-income countries is to provide
women with the means to have control of their bodies. Over
50 per cent of married women in Africa say they want to
avoid pregnancy, but nearly 50 per cent of them say they
are not using modern methods to prevent it. That translates
to some 85 million married women who say they want to
avoid pregnancy but are not deploying modern methods of
birth control. Other things remaining the same, the number
will increase from 85 million to 100 million women by 2030.
That is the size of the unmet need for family planning in the
region. Implications for the region's future population size
are all too easy to draw.

Indifference toward demography as a factor in sustainable
development is reflected in the Organisation for Economic

Co-operation and Development (OECD)'s practice of allocating less than 1 per cent of its aid budget to family planning and reproductive health. The World Bank also attaches low priority to it. Moreover, African countries relegate family planning to minor government departments. It is insidious for international organisations and national governments to seek to empower women while neglecting to offer the services women need to exercise control over their own bodies by spacing pregnancies and choosing their family size. It is even more insidious for development and environmental charities to support that neglect by avoiding discussions on the subject.

CHAPTER 7

Pay for What You Use

In *The Economics of Welfare*, an early twentieth-century book that introduced the study of environmental externalities, the economist A.C. Pigou used a home-grown example of a unidirectional adverse externality (the action of one party adversely affecting another) to show that they are a sign of weak property rights (the affected party is not compensated).

A close variant of the example he used is that of a firm regularly discharging untreated waste into a river. Pigou argued that the harm caused by the discharge should be measured as the loss in social wellbeing (perhaps the sum of individual wellbeings; Pigou was a Utilitarian) and he thought that to eliminate the adverse externality requires a 'visible hand'. His notion of a visible hand was 'government', so he introduced the idea of pollution taxes. The government would then read social wellbeing in terms of the expressed views of citizens and then estimate the appropriate level of tax. The idea is for the (Utilitarian) government to impose a tax on the firm sufficiently stiff that it takes steps to reduce damage to a minimum acceptable level, judged in terms of the increase in social wellbeing. That would in turn also reduce the quantity of provisioning goods that the economy draws on to produce GDP.

The minimum acceptable level of harm could also be implemented by regulation. In that case, there would be no financial transfer between the firm and the regulator. The pollution tax could, of course, be set so high that the firm finds it in its interest to treat its waste completely. In the latter case, the tax would resemble a regulation, an outright prohibition. Therein lies one difference between taxation and regulation: in one case, there is financial transfer from the firm to the regulator; in the other, there is none.

The other difference between taxation and regulation is more subtle. It has to do with differences in what agencies know about themselves and the world at large. It would seem plausible to imagine that a firm has a better idea of its production costs than a regulator does. If the regulator imposes a tax, it does so without full knowledge of the firm's production costs and cannot exactly predict what the firm's pollution discharge will be in response. The public will therefore be uncertain about the level of pollution. In contrast, if the regulator was to impose a quantity restriction – for example, an outright ban on pollution – the public would know what to expect, but the firm's production costs would remain hidden from them.

The Pigouvian tax eliminates the adverse externality in question, but what of the fact that the firm now charges more for their product? It is a fundamental insight of economists to have uncovered ways by which the tax revenue could be used by government so that everyone benefits. The government, for example, could use the revenue to supply more public goods than it currently does.

Political Engagement

However, to assume that, once a polity has identified the ideal solution it knows what to do, would be a mistake. Determining and then enforcing a Pigouvian tax comes at the end of a political process, and the process itself is likely to differ from context to context. Details matter. Experience tells us that the government will need to be informed of the pollution and then be lobbied before the public can expect action. But civic activity is not costless, in time if in nothing else. Moreover, pollution in the river is non-excludable, meaning that even those parties who don't join know they would enjoy an unpolluted river if the lobbying by others was successful. There is then a temptation to free ride – the higher the personal cost of the civic activity, the greater the temptation. If individuals' informed preferences were sufficiently similar and their personal costs nearly identical, the temptation would be much the same for all, which means no one would engage in lobbying, and the river would remain polluted. This is a standard argument in game theory.

Fortunately, people are not the same. The costs of social engagement as well as the weight someone places on an unpolluted river system differ from person to person. Those with low costs and strong feelings would begin the movement, encouraging others to join by pointing to the mutual benefits of collective action. Informing and persuading recalcitrant neighbours is vital at this stage. If, with luck, enough people were to join the coalition, the local authority would be obliged to take note. But even then, there can be hurdles, depending on how responsive various arms of government are to citizens' complaints. The denial by scientists employed by the fossil fuel industry even a few years ago that carbon emissions are responsible for global climate change tells us that the firm in our example would hire experts to argue that the pollution was harmless. The dispute might then go to the courts. How *that* pans out would depend in part on the finances available to the citizens' action group to employ lawyers. And so on.

This helps explain why so many harmful externalities go unattended to for long periods of time, even in otherwise democratic societies; many are never touched. However, an understanding among citizens that, on such matters as public health, there should be regulations on companies handling waste would be in line with contemporary thinking in rich democratic societies. The belief is that people have the right to a clean river. In poor countries, especially those with weak governance, de facto property rights would go the other way round, and the public would take it as given that the firm has the right to pollute the river.

Despite all the caveats, Pigouvian taxes under various guises are not unfamiliar today. In the UK, customers in retail shops are obliged to pay a price (10p currently) for every plastic bag they request to carry their shopping.

Vehicle emission charges in city centres help to keep the air breathable. But these taxes are not imposed in most places. Microplastics everywhere enter the marine food chain and travel thousands of miles, and there are cities you want to avoid if you value your lungs. Provided a society is rich, the latter pollution is controllable. But while the examples could suggest that the way to overcome ecological problems is for societies to pursue GDP growth and thereby finance Nature restoration via Pigouvian taxation – and they have been so read in prominent publications – they are wholly unrepresentative. The use of plastic bags and the emission of fumes that blight a city's air require the extraction of provisioning goods, and indirectly make additional demands for maintenance and regulating services. The Impact Inequality tells us that the larger is GDP per capita, the bigger is the ecological footprint.

Pigou's solution is simpler to put to work within national boundaries than it is when externalities cross national borders. Then, an added layer of negotiations is involved: nations. To revive the dead zone in the Gulf of Mexico would require cooperation between the US federal government and the various state governments of the region through which the Mississippi–Missouri river system flows. It would also require strong complaints from those who suffer damage owing to the dead zones. Eliminating transboundary externalities is especially hard; the protracted international negotiations at the Conference of the Parties (COP) over global climate change and biodiversity loss are witness to that.

Payment for Ecosystem Services

Pigou's reasoning transfers easily to cases of beneficial externalities; activities that have unaccounted-for beneficial consequences should be subsidised to coax people to undertake
more of those activities that give rise to them. Pigouvian
subsidies improve the efficiency with which resources are
allocated – that is, they reduce the quantity of provisioning
goods that the global economy draws on to produce GDP
(they increase α) in the Impact Inequality. The UK government pays farmers to grow hedgerows that can serve as
nesting places for birds and insects and raise local biodiversity. The practice, widely known as 'payment for ecosystem
services', is increasingly being adopted. China, Costa Rica
and Mexico, for example, have also initiated programmes in
which landowners receive payment for furthering biodiversity conservation, carbon sequestration, landscape amenities
and hydrological services. The payment is usually made by
the government from general taxation.

There are variations on the theme. Watersheds purify the
water flowing through them. If the benefits downstream of
a watershed go unacknowledged, the incentive to develop
it upstream for residential and commercial use can be high.
Pigou's solution for this case would be a tax on construction
upstream and for the local authority to invest in restoring
the ecology of the watershed. But there are usually many
parties in a Pigouvian programme. Restoration of the Catskills watershed in the state of New York, which provides

residents of New York City with clean water, is an example. By the 1980s, urban development had damaged the watershed to the extent that water available to the city from reservoirs was showing signs of becoming undrinkable. One solution was to construct a water purification plant as a substitute for the watershed, but estimates suggested that to be more expensive than restoring the Catskills, by something like a 4:1 ratio. An agreement reached in 1997 between the New York City Department of Environmental Protection, the federal government and the Catskills area committees led to a restoration of the watershed. Among other measures, land was purchased so that its use could be restricted, sewage treatment plants were constructed, and farmers were compensated for any voluntary improvement they made to prevent animal and chemical waste from entering the water system. The water that residents of New York City drink is now drawn from reservoirs collecting the Catskills streams.

There are charities that initiate movements to restore Nature, though they differ enormously across the globe.[*] The UK's 46 Wildlife Trusts create Nature reserves – currently some 2,300 reserves covering more than 100,000 hectares – often by purchasing farmland and working with local authorities, developers, farmers and local businesses. The reserves attract wildflowers and offer a sanctuary to species of insects, birds and such animals as voles and beavers that are disappearing from water bodies. And they offer green spaces to the 85 per cent of the UK's population who live in urban

---

* Viewed from the perspective of the Impact Inequality, restoring Nature raises her combined regeneration rate (G).

centres. Currently, the Wildlife Trusts have nearly a million members and are supported by some 40,000 volunteers.

In Assam, India, the Balipara Foundation, a Nature conservation charity, works with rural and indigenous forest communities in the foothills of the eastern Himalayas. Annual reports from the foundation speak of a combination of factors that led to the erosion of natural capital in the region. Indifference shown by the state government made it hard for communities to combat rising uncertainties in vegetable and crop production in the face of climate change. Although the region has been experiencing more rainfall, it arrives in short bursts, causing land erosion and floods. That has limited the recharge of groundwater. Declining incomes have encouraged people to clear forests for agriculture, which has then led to a deterioration in key maintenance and regulating services – soil and water quality were affected especially. Meanwhile, the population has grown, and that has led to yet further pressure on the forests, heightening historical tensions among communities. Militias have been felling trees and selling timber to finance their operation. The Balipara Foundation has tried to break the cycle by creating economic opportunities for local people, encouraging communities to assume stewardship in habitat restoration. More than 100,000 trees have been planted by them in depleted forest patches. Agroforestry in the region has been diversified; local people now grow fruit, vegetables and herbs for export to neighbouring markets. There is a long way to go, but the example illustrates the role Nature conservation charities can play in reviving local ecosystems.

Then there are initiatives on Nature conservation that are

Migratory ducks in California wetlands of the central San Joaquin Valley at the Merced National Wildlife Refuge, California (Alamy)

easy to overlook because they are unusual. The Central Valley of California is a flyway for American migratory birds such as waders, but over 90 per cent of California's wetlands have given way to agriculture and urban development. Flooded rice fields provide food sources and rest areas for shorebirds, but rice farmers flood their land in winter, which does not coincide with the annual visit by waders. Instead of purchasing land and flooding it for the avian visitors, The Nature Conservancy (TNC), a global Nature conservation charity, ran a reverse auction in 2014, where farmers submitted bids specifying the duration and area of farmland they would flood and the price at which they would do it. TNC chose the best bids in terms of their ecological value. The auction would seem to have had a significant impact. Shorebird species richness was three times greater and average shore-bird density was five times greater in fields that were winners in the auction than in similar non-participating fields.

Norm-guided Governance

Matters are different in the case of local ecosystems. Village ponds, grazing fields, threshing grounds, woodlands, marshes and coastal fisheries are within the purview of people inhabiting them. Can communities avoid the tragedy of the commons there? If they can, how?

In times past, when people lived in closely knit communities, they depended entirely on social norms of behaviour to protect individual and collective interests, but adherence to norms requires that one's actions are *observable* by others. If they are, then those interests can be protected and promoted through mutual enforcement.

Norms are conditional acts: 'Do A if B happens, do C otherwise'; 'Do X if she does Y, do Z otherwise', and so forth. These sentences, simple though they appear to be, can hide elaborate strictures. Breaches of acceptable behaviour, for example, could be met with punishment – say, a fine or expressions of disapproval, maybe even social sanctions – meaning that norms include in them strictures for imposing penalties when the situation calls for them. Mutual enforcement of norms in times past was the means of living within bounds of what today would be called a 'social contract'.

The *raison d'être* of norms is the need in all societies, past or present, to practise reciprocity: 'I take only my fair share of fish from the lake, while observing that you are harvesting your fair share.' Reciprocity also includes the flipside of behaviour, as a failure to reciprocate provides a justification for the other parties to withhold cooperation on the next occasion. A norm assumes the form of a *social* norm if it is in the interest of each member of a community to act in accordance with it when *all others* in the community act in accordance with it. Game theorists call that situation a social equilibrium.

Self-confirming beliefs hold social equilibria in place. People trust one another to carry out what they said they would, even what is expected of them to do, because in a social equilibrium people are confident that the norms that are in place provide the required incentives for people to act in accordance with them. Communities lived by norms in the past to further their projects and purposes (although they would not necessarily have put it that way) and, as we will see presently, they do so even today.

Norms are not written down. We learn our society's norms from our earliest years, observing behaviour and the responses by others to our behaviour. Family and neighbours traditionally served as the school where we learned the norms guiding our society, which is why visitors from afar are sometimes at sea as to how to behave in public – they are unfamiliar with the local culture.

Social norms include the response expected of others when a community member has acted in a wrong way, which, as mentioned, may require payment of a fine, but it could be non-monetary; for example, being subjected to social disapproval, perhaps even a sanction (the practice of shunning someone found guilty of a misdemeanour is widespread, though we don't usually use the word any longer). Likewise, social norms can include rewards for good behaviour, receiving praise from others or enjoying an elevated social status. Counterfactual reasoning is involved when we ask ourselves what others would say and do if we were to act otherwise.

All that granted, it should not be thought that the mutual beliefs held together in social equilibrium could be held up in a court of law. We are including here tacit understandings, especially those that are enshrined in what one might call the community's culture, of what is appropriate behaviour and what is not.

Modern urban societies, in contrast, rely greatly on the state to enforce agreements between people. Environmental law is the arena one points to when a company is found polluting a river. But as the law requires that claims and counterclaims of litigants are *verifiable*, court cases are expensive. Which is why the bedrock of even the most modern of societies is built on social norms, for if nothing else, the law itself depends for its legitimacy on its general acceptance by citizens. And the latter requires a shared understanding of civic life, which brings us back to the salience of social norms.

I do not know of any empirical study that asks whether people's dependence on the law relative to social norms increases in the process of economic development. What I *do* know is that rural people in low-income countries depend far more on social norms than the law as they go about their lives. One reason is that the courts can be far from reach. Another is more of a speculation on my part. For those living interdependent lives, as people relying heavily on their local ecosystem do, using the law against someone would go against the sense of fellow-feeling that is acquired through repeated compliance with the norms of their community.

Common Property Resources

Implicit in social norms is a mutual understanding of the way provisioning goods from the local ecosystem should be shared. That enables communities to prevent the tragedy of the commons.

Communitarian governance of local ecosystems is widely practised even today. It is self-evidently practised among small indigenous groups that live in forests and mountain habitats, largely detached from trade with outsiders. Their dependence on their local ecosystems is complete and it is essential for them that social norms regarding resource use, inherited and adapted from the distant past, are adhered to tightly. Being poor, they enjoy no slack. Errors in compliance can mean extinction.

But communitarian systems of governance are also practised among farming and fishing communities in the world's poorer regions, even those that are otherwise embedded in market systems. Anthropologists, economists and political scientists have discovered that village ponds, woodlands, marshes, coastal fisheries, meadows, grazing fields, mangrove forests and water holes are in many instances neither private nor state property but are not open access either. They are communal property, which is why they are known as 'common property resources', or CPRs.

Agricultural land, especially in densely populated areas, in contrast, is usually not a common property resource. There is a reason for that. Creating agricultural land requires investment, transforming diverse ecosystems into fields that are uniform as far as the eye can see. Farmers would be tempted to free ride on investment and operating costs if agricultural land was a CPR. Weak incentives would lead to stagnation, even decay. The experience with collective farms in what was previously the Soviet Union testifies to that. Those regions of sub-Saharan Africa where land was, until recently, held by kinship were exceptions, but only because land was plentiful in the past and because poor soil quality meant that land had to be kept fallow for extended periods.*

Under norm-based management, community members are restricted in what they can harvest from their common property resource, and outsiders are barred from entry. Transactions involving their products are mostly not mediated by market prices, which is why they are not reported in national economic accounts. But they have been, and are, an essential feature of life among rural people in agrarian societies.

Because communitarian practices have important social

---

* Of course, it may be that agricultural productivity remained low there *because* land was held by kinship, not by individuals. As elsewhere in the social sciences, causation typically works in both directions.

functions, such as avoiding the tragedy of the commons, scholars in their writings often display a sense of reverence for communities managing their common property resources. But the reverence should be tempered. People living on CPRs suffer from inequities just as people in cosmopolitan societies do, even if the discriminated groups differ. Studies have found that women often don't have equal access to their CPRs. In India, caste Hindus have privileged access. It is important to study communitarian governance not because they are necessarily egalitarian, but because they have been known to manage local ecosystems more efficiently than state-supported market-based systems.

Are common property resources important in agrarian societies today? In a pioneering work, the economist Narpat S. Jodha found evidence from dry rural districts in central India that the proportion of income among poor households based directly on CPRs was 15–25 per cent. Others have arrived at even larger estimates. In a sample of villages in Zimbabwe, the proportion of income based directly on CPRs was found to be 35 per cent, the figure for the poorest being 40 per cent. Among indigenous populations, deep in the forests, the figure can be near 100 per cent.

As a proportion of total assets in a village community, CPRs range widely across ecological zones. They have been found to be most prominent in arid regions, mountain regions and unirrigated areas; they are least prominent in humid regions and river valleys. There is a rationale behind this, based on the need to pool risks. Woodlands, for example, are spatially inhomogeneous ecosystems. In some years, one group of plants bears fruit in one part of a woodland, in other years some other group in some other part is fecund. Relative to average output, fluctuations are larger in arid regions, mountain regions and unirrigated areas. If a woodland was to be divided into private parcels, each household would face greater risks than it would under communal ownership and self-regulation. The reduction in individual household risks could be small, but as average incomes were (and still are) very low in poor villages, household benefits from communal ownership would be large.

Arrangements for an equal distribution of the products of CPRs is a subtle matter to devise if the productivity of sites fluctuates over time. Rotation of access to the best site is an example of how this can be achieved. It is often practised in relation to coastal fisheries, fuel reserves in forest land and fodder sites in grasslands. Rotation enables users to get a fair share.

It would be possible in principle for the community to parcel out the local ecosystem as private property and encourage households to take out insurance. But that move would jeopardise cooperation in other activities for at least two reasons. First, cooperation has been found to be habit forming; so, dispensing with cooperation in any one activity could lead to a weakening of cooperation in other activities. Second, cooperation is more robust when sanctions for opportunism in any one venture include exclusions not only from that venture, but also from other collective ventures. Abandoning cooperation in one field of activity thus reduces the robustness of cooperation in other fields of activity. It explains why relationships are so frequently tied to one another in rural communities. If you fail to cooperate over sharing provisioning goods from the CPR, your neighbours won't look kindly at you when you need a loan.

Common property resources not only supply households with a regular flow of provisioning goods (water, fuelwood, fibres, building material, fruit, honey, fish), they also offer a fallback position in times of crop failure. Studies have found households on the margin of survival to make more trips into the forest for non-timber products when times are hard. CPRs are sometimes the only assets to which the otherwise disenfranchised, such as the landless, have access. For example, a study in Maranhão, Brazil, found *babassu* products drawn from CPRs to be of especial significance among landless people. Extraction from the plants offers support to the poorest of the poor, most especially women.

The character of ecosystems is inevitably site specific. Ponds even in neighbouring villages in what may appear to be a homogeneous landscape, as in the wetlands of Bangladesh, are not the same. Each has distinctive features depending on soil quality, slope, microclimate and so forth. Villagers have greater knowledge of those details than government ecologists. Forest inhabitants in the foothills of the Himalayas and the Andes know more about the nitty-gritty of life and death among animals and plants in their locale than professors of ecology or forest rangers from urban centres. Inhabitants may not have knowledge of the discipline of ecology, but that is a different matter. In a study on forest conservation in the central Himalayas, the economist E. Somanathan and his colleagues found that tree density was significantly higher in sites that were managed by village councils than in areas where the state was involved in forest management. Subsequent studies on the management of wildlife and irrigation have found that devolution of responsibilities from the state to local communities leads to more efficient resource management.

Cooperation doesn't appear in a vacuum. In the contemporary world there is a potential role for government and charities (non-government organisations, or NGOs) in helping to build or rebuild local institutions through which communities get to realise the advantages of collective action. Such help would involve, among other things, devising clearly defined rules concerning the allocation of burdens and benefits, rules whose compliance can be observed (hopefully, verified also) by the others involved.

In a study in northwest India, the economists Kanchan Chopra and S.C. Gulati found that distress migration (which usually refers to leaving your home area due to desperation or coercion) out of villages where charities had been at work to create institutions for managing water and pastureland on a communitarian basis was lower than in villages where there had been little attempt to create such institutions. Significantly, the authors found that the incidence of participation in communal pastureland was higher among villagers who were participating in communal water-management schemes than among villagers who were not. That suggests once again that cooperation begets cooperation.

Local Ecosystems and Ecological Risks

Common property resources have deteriorated in recent years in many regions of the world, further impoverishing the inhabitants that remain there. There is an enormous literature identifying reasons why. Here are four examples that show how communal management systems can be eroded via diverse channels.

The economist Pranab Mukhopadhyay conducted a historical study of the transformation of agrarian land in Goa, India, that was earlier owned and regulated by a communitarian institution called the *communidades*. When Goa became a part of India, the government introduced land reforms that gave tenants the right to purchase the land they had worked. Mukhopadhyay doesn't question the underlying motivation behind land reforms, but notes one unfortunate consequence, which is the breakdown of cooperation among households in maintaining the embankments that had earlier prevented the land from flooding by tidal waters. Over the years, deterioration of the embankments has led to an increase in soil salinity. This is a case of a defendable public policy having unintended adverse consequences.

Another channel through which CPRs can deteriorate is communal rights being overturned by central fiat. To establish its political authority, several states in the Sahel in North Africa imposed rules in the 1980s that destroyed communal management practices in the forests. Villages ceased to have the authority to enforce sanctions on those who broke communitarian rules. But state officials didn't have the expertise to manage the commons, and often they were corrupt.

Eroding ecosystems and high population growth lead communities to demand provisioning goods increasingly from their local ecosystems. In a remarkable anthropological study, Roger Blench has examined one such pathway by which communities fall into poverty traps. He recounts a battle for resources between pastoralists and farmers in contemporary North-Central Nigeria, which has among the highest fertility rates of Nigeria, a country that has undergone unparalleled demographic growth. The conflict has meant farmers having to enter ever more marginal land, particularly to riverine areas, where cattle grazing has been replaced by dry-season horticulture. Farmers are in addition engaged in cutting trees for wood-fuel and timber. Deforestation of riverbanks has led to soil erosion and reduced agricultural yields. Meanwhile, pastoralists who migrate seasonally have placed the remaining open land under greater grazing pressure owing to population growth. The vegetation of the semi-arid zone has in consequence undergone significant changes.* Plant and animal species characteristic of the region have been moving further south and colonising new ecological niches in the subhumid zone. Pastoralists with livestock varieties adapted to the vegetation of the Sahel have been moving south, not only because grazing

---

* Reduced rainfall should be added to this, but there is an identification problem as regards the cause: climate change and/or altered vegetation cover arising from land-use changes.

prospects are under pressure in their home landscape, but also because new pastures have been released, as resident pastoralists in the subhumid region turn further south. The conjunction of a high density of farms and constant waves of pastoralists moving into each ecozone where they have no traditional relationships has inevitably resulted in conflicts with farmers. The practice of social norms, a mainstay of traditional societies, are disappearing under the strain. So long as these ecological factors remain unrecognised and remedies are not sought, conflict can be expected to renew itself constantly, and no amount of effort at reconciliation will have an impact on these waves of migration.

Wackernagel and his collaborators have estimated that Nigeria's provisioning goods relative to its capacity to supply them on a sustainable basis is in the range of 1.5 to 2, even while many of its citizens live in great poverty. The country is an exporter of fossil fuels, whose extraction is especially prone to inflicting environmental damages on the locality. There are no estimates of the wealth that is leaking out from Nigeria to importing countries on an annual basis, but our previous discussion tells us that there must be some and that it is contributing to the high ecological overreach of 1.5 to 2.

CHAPTER 8

A New Measure of Wealth

The public viewpoint of our place in Nature prompts three types of enquiries.

The most familiar one seeks to find the course of actions public decision makers should take. Imagine that we have our gaze on our national economy. A problem we would be interested in is determining how much of the nation's GDP ought to be devoted to consumption and how the remainder should be invested – much like the passive investor we considered earlier, who juggles his portfolio, seeking assets with the best risk-adjusted rates of return.

Here we are considering the same problem but from the perspective of a different agency. We want the decision makers in our economy to choose investment projects whose motivation should differ from that of the private investor. But they face a problem. The provisioning goods in ecosystems that are open access have no market prices (they are free goods), a fact that explains why natural capital has given way to produced capital in investment decisions throughout the world. But even though the provisioning goods may have no assigned commercial value, they have social value.

That markets undervalue natural capital is not limited

to open access ecosystems. They undervalue it wherever consumption or investment activities give rise to externalities. The rate of species extinctions and the likely size of the Impact Inequality tell us that the global economy ought to tilt its investment portfolio toward natural capital, away from produced capital. The account of Pigouvian taxes and subsidies pointed to the direction in which we would want decision makers in our economy to move. And we feel they should recognise that the *social* profitability of investment projects differs from *private* profitability. But that tells us that instead of using market prices, decision makers should use *notional* prices to calculate the profitability of investment projects.

To illustrate a notional price (economists call it the 'accounting price', which we mentioned in Chapter 4 in relation to assessing the 'weight' of the demands we make on provisioning goods, and will discuss later in this chapter), consider the largest mammals of all: whales. In countries that permit whale hunting, a whale's market price reflects the commercial value of its oil and meat – a large whale fetches some 20,000 to 40,000 US dollars. That's the value of a dead whale. But whales are also a store of carbon. A recent publication from the International Monetary Fund (IMF) used estimates of the social cost of carbon to show that the notional price of a live whale can be more than a million US dollars. To be sure, this is not whales' intrinsic value (i.e., their own fundamental value, independent of external factors), but pointing to their large instrumental value (i.e., the value of their broader usefulness to our own objectives) may protect whales more securely than insisting that they have an intrinsic value as living organisms.

The second kind of enquiry for someone adopting the public viewpoint asks how social wellbeing in their society compares with social wellbeing in other societies. Variants of this are a common subject for study. The World Bank, the OECD and the UN Development Programme, among other international organisations, routinely make cross-country comparisons of the standard of living. The most common measure in use is, as one might expect, GDP per capita. Countries are ranked on that basis, and even the distinction between developed and less-developed countries is most frequently based on countries' GDP per capita. But because of widespread criticism of the practice of relying on a single measure, international organisations in recent years have gone beyond per capita GDP and now regularly compare countries in terms of such measures as adult literacy, life expectancy, income inequality, level of corruption, civil and political liberties, and so on. The latter measures go beyond livings standards to reflect something like the quality of life.

The third kind of enquiry asks whether there have been improvements in social wellbeing over time. Often, studies of this kind are retrospective, as in the Maddison data on changes in global per capita GDP and life expectancy. But they can be prospective too, as in asking whether, under current policies, social wellbeing in a country is likely to be greater in, say, five years' time than it is today. International organisations routinely conduct such studies, and they are the basis on which people assess the progress and regress of nations.

Most frequently, per capita GDP is the measure deployed for this purpose as well, but it is especially unsuited for the task. First, GDP is a flow (so many billions of dollars *per year*), and flows can tell us nothing about what lies ahead, only stocks can. Second, the 'G' in the acronym GDP is 'gross', meaning that GDP does not deduct the depreciation of capital that accompanies production and consumption.

Despite its obvious weaknesses, GDP as a measure is here to stay. Just as a household with a lot of cash in hand enjoys an advantage in many manners of speaking than a household that does not, a large GDP enables a nation to manoeuvre itself in the economic world – for example, tilting the terms of trade in its favour and getting other countries to see its ways. There is in consequence a race among nations, each seeking to beat others in its GDP figure, which is an international version of the race to conspicuous consumption among individuals.

And that brings us full circle back to the point we noted in Chapter 4, that economic development in the Anthropocene has seen an enormous increase in produced and human capital, and a massive depreciation of natural capital. GDP is insensitive to this line of thinking.

The idea is not to dismiss GDP from economic reasoning – GDP is useful for short-run macroeconomics management – but to create a parallel system of capital accounts, akin to firms' balance sheets, for judging economic performance over time, as a means of addressing the fact that we have accumulated produced capital and human capital in the Anthropocene but have degraded natural capital to an extent that we have been endangering our collective futures.

The Idea of Sustainable Development

In a now-classic publication of 1987, officially titled *Our Common Future* but known as the Brundtland Report, the World Commission on Environment and Development shifted the terms in which the last of the three types of enquiries on our list are framed, and it defined 'sustainable development' as development that meets the needs of the present without compromising the ability of future generations to meet their own needs. I don't know of another idea in growth and development economics and the economics of poverty that caught the imagination of the public as quickly as the notion of sustainable development did, but it deserved its immediate acceptance as a tool for thinking about economic possibilities for the future.

The Brundtland criterion asks us to compare economic opportunities at different points in time and defines sustainable development to be paths along which those opportunities expand continually (or, more accurately, don't ever contract). Because we shouldn't expect there to be a unique sustainable development path – the criterion does not distinguish the composition of capital assets on the many potential paths along which opportunities expand continually – we would need additional criteria to be able to choose among them. The Brundtland criterion can thus be thought of as a basic requirement, nothing more.

Advocates of economic (read GDP) growth could, of course, respond by insisting that it is *because* GDP growth creates economic opportunities that national governments should pursue it. But in defining the notion of sustainable development as it did, the Brundtland Report hinted that opportunities are embodied in stocks of capital assets, not in flows of incomes.

As capital stocks are an economy's productive base, the available set of options at any date depends on the portfolio of assets the economy holds at that date. Just as the acquisition of human capital (health, education, skills, aptitude, character) is a means for people to expand their life opportunities, enlargement of an economy's portfolio of capital stocks creates greater opportunities for the economy. The Brundtland criterion for sustainable development can thus be interpreted as development along which an economy's portfolio of assets expands over time.

But assets differ, which means the mix of assets in an economy's portfolio matters – a mere head count of assets won't do. It could be that to expand a nation's economic opportunities, decision makers should disinvest in some assets and invest in other more productive assets. Moreover, opportunities themselves differ in their attractiveness. So, the Brundtland criterion requires an ethical dimension, involving the *social worth* of assets. This it did not provide; it was left for others to fill those large blanks.

As mentioned, notional prices in economic accounting are also called *accounting prices*. Formally, the accounting price of a good or service is the contribution that an additional unit of it would make to social wellbeing, other things remaining the same. Estimating accounting prices therefore involves counterfactual reasoning. Because the economy moves through time, social wellbeing at any time also includes the wellbeing of future people. We can call our moving conception of social wellbeing, 'wellbeing across the generations'. It is not a Platonic object but represents an evaluative judgement made by the person who has assumed the public viewpoint.

Accounting prices combine the possible and the desirable. The 'possible' is reflected in the economic projection on which decision makers are to base their estimates of accounting prices.* The 'desirable' appears in the conception of wellbeing across the generations we deploy to reflect our values when assuming the public viewpoint. And the public viewpoint can be adopted by a person regardless of the character of the society she studies. Accounting prices are thus 'all things considered' judgements.

An asset's accounting price is not fixed. As an economy's asset composition changes over time, so do the accounting prices of the assets, in effect reflecting shifts in the assets' composition. To estimate prices, decision makers need to make a forecast of the economy's future. Economic models are essential for doing that. Organisations rely on models of their economies, including data on their asset base, quantitative information about production and consumption possibilities, and assumptions about institutions, the public knowledge base, the human motivations in play, and so

---

* There is no presumption that the economy is well managed; accounting prices are as relevant in well-ordered societies as in dysfunctional ones.

on. National banks, ministries of finance and international economic organisations make such forecasts all the time. Each organisation has its own economic model, reflecting its reach and competence.

As always, problems of measurement circumscribe what we can include on our list of capital stocks. I have constructed the three-way classification of capital assets (produced capital, human capital, natural capital), and have excluded all other forms of capital because of the constraints that measurement problems impose on decision makers. In what follows, I first discuss ways to estimate accounting prices and then explain how such intangible assets as institutions and knowledge, missing though they are in our classification, can be incorporated in our economic reasoning.

To illustrate accounting prices, it helps to start with a thoroughly mundane example of a piece of produced capital: the desk at which I am typing this chapter. The desk's accounting price today depends on its possible future uses. As I am typing the chapter in my study in Cambridge, I would imagine its accounting price differs from that of a similar desk in a war-torn country (it is most likely to be higher here). In general, accounting prices of desks reflect their *use* value. But not invariably, for if the desk had been left to me by my father, it's worth to me would have been higher than its mere use value. It would have included the desk's *intrinsic* value to me.

But the desk also has a market price. The price I paid couldn't have exceeded the desk's use value to me, otherwise I wouldn't have bought it. However, the market price could have been, and in all probability was, less than its use value to me, the difference being the 'surplus' in my wellbeing I enjoy from having purchased it.

And that gives us a strong clue where to start when estimating accounting prices. Should an asset, or one similar, have a market price, we could begin with that and add (or subtract) the value of externalities that are likely to be associated with its use. The desk's production probably created externalities, but they would have been bygones for society when I saw it in the department store. Accounting prices are forward looking.

There is now an enormous literature on methods for estimating the accounting price of items of human capital. Interestingly, the earliest attempts were directed at valuing labour effort in what were then seen largely to be non-wage-based agrarian economies with surplus labour. Today, the focus is on human capital and the activities people are capable of undertaking. To make the analysis manageable, human capital is taken in these exercises to be the value of a person's lifetime supply of labour. Wages and salaries are interpreted as returns on human capital. Reducing someone to a mere earner could seem crass, but we are studying the productivity of human capital, not the person's moral status.

Accounting Prices of Natural Capital

Measurement problems are a reason we have avoided any mention of quantifying Nature's supply of maintenance and regulating services thus far. It is perhaps fortunate, then, that because of the tensions that exist between humanity's demand for provisioning goods and Nature's ability to supply maintenance and regulating services, ecological economists have been able to develop the idea of natural capital solely on the backs of provisioning goods because they can be measured. Even water quality is measurable quantitatively (e.g., water's pH level).

Provisioning goods possess two kinds of value that have been much discussed by environmental economists: *use value* and *amenity value*.

Use Value

Consider first the use value of provisioning goods. If the goods are open access, their market price would be zero, in which case we must start from scratch. That's how economists proceed when estimating the accounting price of CO_2 in the atmosphere. They embed the climate system in an otherwise standard economic model of growth and development, and ask in which ways future global consumption would be affected if an additional unit of CO_2 was emitted into the atmosphere. The effect is the small reduction in future consumption of provisioning goods because of a marginal increase in CO_2. That's the accounting price of CO_2. Because it is negative, the accounting price is called the *social cost* of CO_2.

In estimating the use value of ecosystems, economists ask after their productivity in supplying provisioning goods. In a pioneering work, the economist Edward Barbier explored the use value of tropical wetlands by identifying the services they provide by supplying provisioning goods.

To do that, the author studied the dynamics of tropical wetlands. The idea was to view a wetland as a production system.

Shrimp (or prawn) farms provide a contrasting illustration. Producing luxury food, shrimp farms are notorious polluters. First, constructing a pond often involves taking bites off mangrove forests and salt marshes, with all the associated losses, including emissions of the carbon previously stored in them. Second, some 30 per cent of shrimp diets are soya, and soya comes from plantations that increasingly fragment tropical forests and eliminate species. Third, the use of antibiotics to keep shrimps healthy pollutes neighbouring waters, including groundwater. Fourth, the working life of a shrimp pond is five to ten years, after which the pond

Aerial view of shrimp farms in Xuân Thủy, Nam Định, Vietnam (Alamy)

is abandoned, while the damaged ecosystems need years longer to recover, assuming they are not further damaged by production activities elsewhere.

Estimating the unaccounted-for damage caused by a shrimp pond is hard work, but it can be done. First, you estimate annual income losses to inhabitants owing to reduced mangrove and marsh cover, to which you add the value of the carbon that was stored in the lost vegetation. You then estimate the annual loss in income from bio-chemical pollution in the adjacent fish nurseries. You will be minded also to include in the calculation that the income benefits from the pond from the export of shrimps will last some five to ten years, but the damaged ecosystem will take years longer to recover. And if you are fastidious, you will add to the market price of soya a figure for the carbon that was stored in the tropical forest cover now lost. Adding all the items across time provides an estimate of the societal rate of return on investment in a shrimp pond. Patently, it is less than the rate of return that you would have estimated were you to have ignored the externalities in your calculation.

Case studies I have read of the ecological economics of shrimp farms in Bangladesh and Vietnam, coordinated by the economist Enamul Haque, don't cover every item on the above list. Even so, they find that the adverse environmental externalities add up to 15–20 per cent of the export prices of shrimp. That means the accounting price of exported shrimp is some 15–20 per cent less than the export price. There is an irony here. The export of shrimp carries with it an implicit subsidy, which should be read as a transfer of wealth from a relatively poor exporting country (Vietnam) to a rich import-ing country (the US).

There are further considerations. Owners of shrimp farms are wealthy and live in urban centres. Those who work on the farms are in contrast impoverished and live locally, which is why and how it is they who bear the brunt of the damage to local ecosystems. So, there is even greater irony in the example; the export of shrimp carries with it an implicit gift from the impoverished in a poor country to the affluent in a rich country. It amounts to a transfer of wealth from the very poor to the rich.

Amenity Value

The Common International Classification of Ecosys-tem Services (see Chapter 1) contains a category, 'Cultural Services', that points to the amenity value of much that is Nature.* Assessing the amenity value involves:

1. *Contingent Valuation Method.* Public goods offer the motivation for a popular valuation method in which representative samples of people are asked hypothetical questions about their willingness to pay for such measures as protecting a species from extinction or designating an ecosystem as a public park. The idea is to add together the individual responses to arrive at an estimate of

---

* Interestingly, environmental economists devised methods for estimating the accounting price of environmental amenities before they turned their attention to the use value of ecosystems.

the willingness-to-pay of the entire population. An alternative is to ask people how much they would be willing to accept as compensation for permitting the amenity to deteriorate from its present state. The idea here, again, is to add up the individual responses to arrive at an estimate of the sum of the willingness-to-accept by the entire population. The two methods taken together are called the *contingent valuation method*, or CVM for short.

There is a big leap from the definition of accounting prices to CVM. The former is the contribution goods and services make to wellbeing across the generations; the latter asks respondents to declare their willingness to pay for them. CVM is attractive because it appeals to our democratic instinct that people should be asked for their opinion on matters that may be of concern to them. The method is attractive also because in principle it can reveal not only an amenity's value, but also respondents' sense of a species' existence value. It is known, for example, that people derive satisfaction from the mere knowledge that the large primates in the forests of Uganda exist, and they do not feel they have to view them. In addition, people have been found to be willing to pay more to prevent an amenity from deteriorating to some specified level or a species from becoming extinct if they are informed that others will contribute as well (a further sign that preferences are socially embedded).

2. *Revealed Preferences for Amenities.* Market prices are usually thought to be the institution *par excellence* where individual preferences are revealed. If you are found purchasing a commodity in the marketplace, it would seem reasonable to conclude that you are willing to pay at least the amount you have paid. Differences in the quality of a marketed good can thus be inferred from differences in prices. For example, the commercial value of residential land has been found to depend on the landscape surrounding it (e.g., the view from the house). A property's *hedonic price* is a measure of its quality.

This line of thought has been extended to determine quality differences in amenities even when they do not have markets. Sites possessing amenity value are often public goods (national parks, beaches). Entry fees limit congestion, but usually they are a small fraction of the cost tourists incur for visiting the sites. That offers a method for estimating the willingness to pay for the amenity: *the cost of travel.* The method has been used widely to study tourism. It could also be used to estimate the value of such national treasures as museums and art galleries for which visitors are not charged an entry fee.

Intangible Infrastructure

What of those intangible assets people refer to as social capital, knowledge capital, institutional capital, and cultural and religious capital? We know they make their presence felt in the Impact Inequality via the quantity of provisioning goods that the global economy draws on to produce GDP, which is how, over time, they influence GDP. But where do they appear in the accounting framework we are constructing here?

We have not included them in the three-way classification of capital goods (produced capital, human capital and natural capital) for a reason. Measurement problems would abound if we were to do so. To see how, consider that if a company issues a fresh order for office chairs, its total number of chairs would become a known multiple of the number today, and that if a person obtains a further year of education, the increase in her human capital would be reflected in the increase in her lifetime earnings. Now consider instead a discovery in the theory of numbers. Fellow mathematicians would no doubt make use of it in their work, but putting a price tag on it, even if it happens to be an accounting price tag, would raise insuperable problems. Academic promotions, prizes for discoveries and other social contrivances offer incentives to researchers to produce work of originality, but that doesn't make fundamental knowledge quantifiable, for it is an intangible public good.

Institutions, including the mutual trust that is required

to make them work, suffer from a similar problem. They are intangible public goods, but we recognise their significance. They are a lubricant that makes societies work. We call those public assets society's *intangible infrastructure*.

In a famous paper of 1957, the economist Robert M. Solow estimated the contribution intangible infrastructure makes to GDP growth,* finding that it far outweighs the contribution produced capital and human capital make to growth (his estimate was a near-90 per cent of GDP growth). But Solow was wary of putting a name to the intangible infrastructure and instead called the near-90 per cent a 'residual,' implying that he wasn't about to say what was contributing so mightily to GDP growth in the US. Since then, economists have unravelled the residual by studying the contribution of new knowledge, or scientific and technical progress, to it. And that provides a clue to how those intangible assets make their presence felt in economic accounting: they influence the accounting prices of capital assets in our three-way classification.

To illustrate this, consider two islands that are identical in every respect bar one: in the first, households trust one another completely; in the second, they distrust one another thoroughly. It is obvious the economic pathways of the two will differ. In the former, households will trade with one another and enjoy the benefits that go with it; in the latter, households will be economically independent of the rest of the world and suffer from all the impediments to progress

---

* Solow studied time series of non-farm gross national income, not GDP, in the US economy.

that come with that. Their economic futures being different, the accounting prices of capital assets in the two island economies at the initial and subsequent dates will be different. As the islands began with an identical asset base, we conclude that even though trust may not be measurable, it will make its presence or absence felt through the structure of accounting prices in the two islands. Some have called an economy's intangible infrastructure its *enabling assets*. They enable the global economy to deploy produced capital, human capital and natural capital for our purposes.

Enabling assets appear in the Impact Inequality in a different form. Recall that the inequality is between our demand for provisioning goods and Nature's combined regeneration rates, which means our intangible infrastructure makes its presence felt in the quantity of provisioning goods that the global economy draws upon to produce GDP (that is, α), and in time on global population and global per capita GDP as well. But there is an ambiguity in how we should interpret the influence of those enabling assets on our wellbeing. The invention of bulldozers has contributed hugely to labour productivity, but it has done so by increasing our reliance on natural capital. The invention has increased the quantity of provisioning goods that the global economy draws upon to produce GDP, and so raises the demand side of the ledger in the Impact Inequality. As the invention is an enabling asset, one could say it has raised the efficiency of labour even as it has reduced the efficiency with which Nature's provisioning goods are deployed for producing the final products that go to make GDP (i.e., reduces α). That's the ambiguity.

Inclusive Wealth

We now have the material we need to put flesh into the Brundtland criterion for sustainable development.

Our task, remember, was to distinguish assets by their social worth and to make use of the accounting value of the mix of assets an economy carries from one date to another. Let us multiply the stock of every capital asset in an economy by its accounting price, and add the accounting values of the stocks. The sum is the economy's wealth as estimated using accounting prices.

The UN Environment Programme (UNEP), which has taken the lead in estimating the wealth of nations, calls the accounting value of an economy's assets its *inclusive wealth*, not simply 'wealth', to highlight that wealth includes the value of natural capital. The Brundtland criterion in effect says that sustainable development is development along which an economy's inclusive wealth increases over time. As all the assets have been valued at their accounting prices, it must be that, along any development path that is sustainable, wellbeing across the generations also increases over time. That means wealth and wellbeing across the generations are two sides of the same normative coin.*

The equivalence between inclusive wealth and wellbeing across the generations is not generally appreciated. For example, the UN SDGs (which we discussed in Chapter 4) were not informed by it. If they had been, the Goals would

---

* This is, of course, not a rigorous proof, but it comes close to one that is.

have been framed in a different way – they would have been about growth in inclusive wealth.

An economy can, in principle, enjoy an increase in inclusive wealth by accumulating produced capital and human capital even while its natural capital is decumulated. That tells us that it is fruitful to decompose inclusive wealth into its three components and study economic history in their light. In an exercise sponsored by UNEP, the economists Shunsuke Managi and Pushpam Kumar estimated changes that took place during 1992–2014 in the composition of global inclusive wealth. They reported that, at accounting prices, the stock of produced capital per capita doubled, human capital per capita increased by some 20 per cent, and natural capital per capita declined by 40 per cent (Fig. 8.1).

FIG. 8.1 GLOBAL CAPITAL STOCKS PER CAPITA 1991–2014

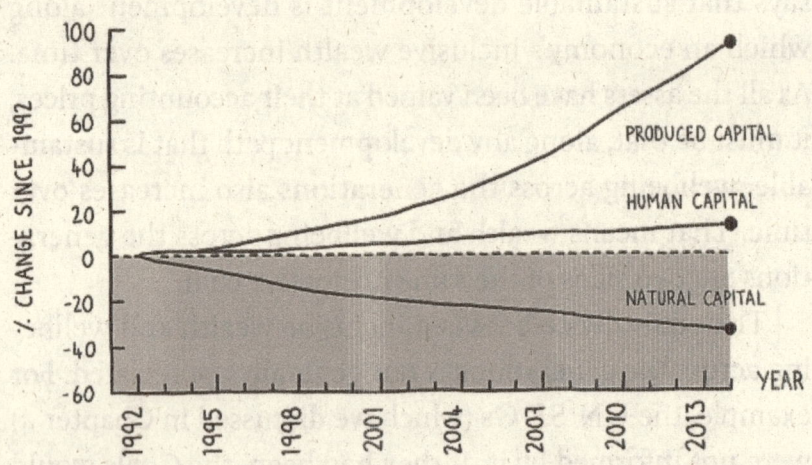

Source: Managi and Kumar (2018)

In the 2022 edition of UNEP's *Inclusive Wealth Report*, the authors reported that in the 30-year period beginning 1992, global inclusive wealth increased by nearly 50 per cent while the stock of global natural capital, valued at accounting prices, declined by 25 per cent. The report concluded, however, that the increase in inclusive wealth did not match the increase in global population in the period: global inclusive wealth per capita therefore declined overall.

If we regard per capita inclusive wealth to be the index we should use for assessing economic progress (and the theorem establishing the equivalence between inclusive wealth and wellbeing across the generations tells us we should), the factors that appear in the Impact Inequality assume enormous significance in our economic future. Policies that could be deployed to close the gap in the Inequality should now be central to global economic thinking.

CHAPTER 9
Policies for Behavioural Change

The Impact Inequality is an accounting statement. It compares the demand we make of the biosphere's provisioning goods – our ecological footprint – and the biosphere's combined regeneration rates, and shows how to express the idea that the former can exceed the latter, which it does today. The Inequality reflects the state of affairs in a period; it does not offer the dynamics that have led to where our global demand and Nature's combined regenerations are now, nor where they are likely to be heading. But we know that if global demand exceeds Nature's combined regeneration rates in this period, the stock of natural capital in the next period will be lower than it is now. The Impact Inequality is therefore a statement about the natural capital component of inclusive wealth. As we noted in the previous chapter, studies published by the UNEP have found not only that natural capital per capita globally has declined in recent years but, more strongly, that global inclusive wealth per capita has also declined. Increases in produced capital and human capital have not compensated for declines in the stock of global natural capital.

Movements over time of inclusive wealth should guide

our reading of the way the human economy is treading the biosphere, but because the current ratio of our global demand for provisional goods to Nature's combined regeneration rates is 1.7, the account of natural capital here has been built round the latter. There are four proximate factors in the Impact Inequality: global population, global per capita GDP, the efficiency with which the global economy draws on provisioning goods to produce GDP (that is, α), and the biosphere's combined regeneration rates. Each affects the others over time, and all are affected by human decisions and the biosphere's responses. If the Inequality is to be reversed, policies should be directed at lowering future global population and global per capita GDP, reducing the quantity of provisioning goods that the global economy draws on to produce GDP, and raising the biosphere's combined regeneration rates. There are several ways in which that could be brought about.

Income Inequality and the Global Ecological Footprint

How does the distribution of incomes affect our global demand for provisioning goods? Or, to put it another way, how does the global income distribution affect the global ecological footprint?

The question is hard to answer because international trade distributes the ecological footprint of nations among one another, and because Nature is mobile. Nevertheless, there are crude estimates that have in varying degrees corrected for those transfers. The Intergovernmental Panel on Climate Change (IPCC) has found that carbon emissions are an increasing function of income. There is a corresponding finding that says ecological footprint is an increasing function of income.

Fig. 9.1, based on the work of Wackernagel and his colleagues, depicts the relationship between per capita GDP and ecological footprint per person drawn from estimates in more than 140 countries. It shows that richer people have larger footprints, but an additional dollar to a rich person leaves behind a smaller footprint than it does if the person were poor.

This is disappointing for anyone who is both an egalitarian and an environmentalist, for it says that if we wish to advocate for more egalitarian distributions of income today

FIG 9.1 ECOLOGICAL FOOTPRINT AND INCOME

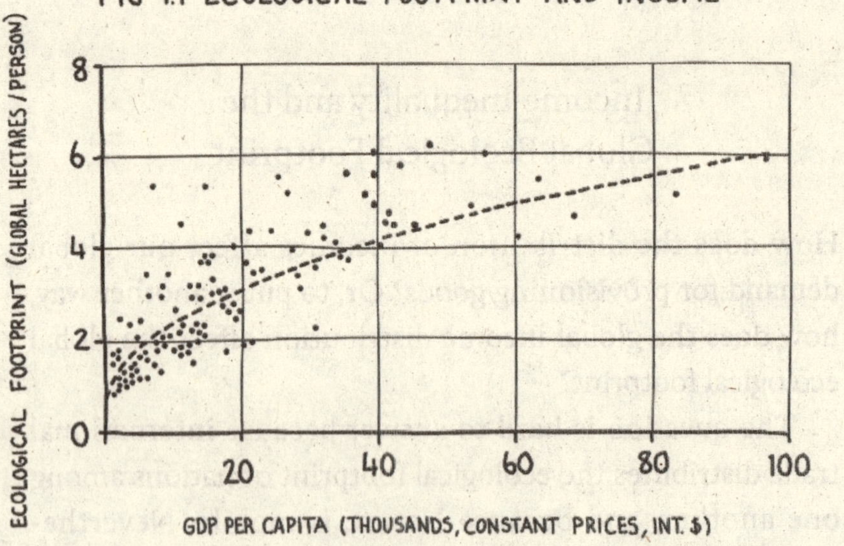

SOURCE: DASGUPTA (2021, 2024)

without further increasing the global ecological overreach, there needs to be a reduction in global GDP. Or to put it in another way, a global GDP with inequality makes less of a demand on the biosphere than the same level of global GDP with complete equality.

Payments for Ecosystem Services

Biodiversity loss stems from institutional failure writ large. Here are three examples that show why our use of the biosphere amounts to pilfering from Nature:

1. *Environmental Subsidies.* The aggregate subsidy humanity pays itself to 'mine' Nature, including subsidies for energy and food production, is of the order of 4–6 trillion US dollars annually, or some 3–5 per cent of global GDP. By raising the quantity of provisioning goods that the global economy draws on to produce GDP (that is, by lowering α), the subsidies create an enormous pressure on the world's ecosystems. These subsidies provide us with a powerful incentive to plunder the biosphere, not preserve it.

2. *Global Commons.* We don't pay for such global public goods as the open seas and tropical rainforests. The former is an open-access resource (we are referring to the seas that lie beyond exclusive economic zones and are not protected zones), suffering from the 'tragedy of the commons',

a classic institutional failure that corresponds to increasing the quantity of provisioning goods that the global economy draws on to produce GDP. Tropical rainforests are a global public good, but are within national jurisdiction, meaning that the benefit a nation would enjoy from preserving them is less than the benefit to humanity. The global community may deplore large-scale decline in the size of the rainforests, but nations that are home to them respond by insisting that their economic development depends on depleting them.

3. *Trade and Wealth Transfers.* Principal exports from tropical regions are primary products, whose extraction inflicts adverse externalities on *local* inhabitants. We noted this when discussing shrimp exports from poor tropical countries. Biodiversity loss is a feature of the externalities. Those losses are not reflected in export prices, meaning that local ecosystems are overexploited. This amounts to a transfer of wealth from the exporting country to the importing country, that is, from a poor country to a rich country. If the emphasis in recent decades on trade liberalisation is anything to go by, such wealth transfers are not acknowledged. Propositions on the benefits of free trade suppose that all goods and services have perfectly competitive markets. In contrast, the economics of biodiversity is about a world where markets are missing for many of Nature's services.

Policies to Reduce the Imbalance

There are clear policy implications arising from these three examples. The moral to be drawn from environmental subsidies is obvious: they encourage people to draw more on provisioning goods to produce GDP than they otherwise would. But perhaps it is *because* the directive is obvious that there have been few attempts at assessing quantitatively the effect on our consumption patterns if the subsidies were removed. On the one hand, an immediate effect would be an increase in commodity prices, and therefore lower disposable incomes; on the other hand, lower taxation stemming from a reduction in subsidies would mean an increase in our disposable incomes. The key point, though, is that removing the subsidies would lead to consumption moving away from Nature-intensive goods. Reduction in the Impact Inequality would trace the change to a combination of changes in per capita GDP, the quantity of provisioning goods that the global economy draws on to produce GDP, and the biosphere's combined regeneration rates.

When considering the global commons, the high seas have received far less attention among national and international decision makers than the atmosphere as a sink for our carbon emissions. But the seas are vital for our existence. There is a need for an institutional mechanism that provides incentives to reduce the pressure we inflict on them from commodity transportation, cruises, fishing, mining and pollutants emanating from land. The standard tools of public economics are regulations and taxes. The former is enshrined in such policies as protected zones, which can be reached by international agreements without the need for an international agency to implement them. That is their attraction. One problem with the schemes is that, even though the open seas are, to use a phrase popular in the 1970s, a 'common heritage of mankind', the benefits from using the oceans for transportation would be enjoyed by users, not by the public.

The latter tool, taxation, has the merit that the rents would in principle accrue to us all. But to implement this mechanism requires an international agency. One possibility would be to establish an agency with the remit to monitor and charge for the use of the high seas (e.g., taxing ocean transportation, mining, deep-sea fishing and the refuse that is deposited into them by nations). That could raise billions of dollars every year, as perhaps a trillion dollars' worth of merchandise is shipped annually across the oceans.

A further rationale for such a taxation scheme is that the rents collected could be used in part to pay nations to conserve the tropical rainforests in their jurisdiction. Currently, the rest of the world complains about the continual destruction of what remains of the world's rainforests, but little is done about it. Payment for ecosystem services is becoming familiar within nations. The idea would be to extend such a payment system to the international sphere.

The proposal has not found enthusiasm among national and international civil servants, on grounds that the world does not have an appetite for that grand an undertaking. (Neither COP26–27 nor COP15, nor for that matter Stockholm 50+, raised the matter.) At the same time, global decision makers at those meetings have expressed the need for the world economy to undergo transformative changes. At the end of the Second World War, nations created the World Bank, the IMF and the UN and its subsidiaries. The post-war US initiative, the Marshall Plan, was designed to lift Europe from the ashes, and it helped to do that. Those were transformative steps. Ashes and rubble are visible, but the silent and invisible processes that are a characteristic of Nature regularly escape our attention.

Trade and wealth transfers tell us that the Global South should *collectively* impose export taxes on primary products. This would ease pressure on their local ecosystems (e.g., rainforests and fisheries) and would also be a source of income for the exporting nations. When the World Trade Promotion Organizations held their 2022 conference in Accra, their brief was to find ways to raise GDP in African countries while encouraging companies to move toward sustainable policies. Yet the event fielded no quantitative models with which to ask whether GDP can be raised even while protecting the region's ecosystems, nor whether companies would adopt ecologically sustainable polices without export taxes. If climate negotiations are taken as illustrative, it would prove hard for African nations to reach collective agreements.

Although exports of primary products involve wealth transfers from exporting to importing countries, it is not an unalloyed benefit for importing countries – the transfers carry with them risks. Investment companies and financial institutions increasingly express concerns over the financial risks that investors experience because of our ecological overreach. Those risks are included in the accounting prices of the assets from which primary products are drawn – the greater the risks, the more the overreach should be avoided, and so, the larger would be the accounting prices of the primary products themselves.

Insuring against such risks in the marketplace is, however, not a viable option, for in addition to the risks that are inevitably present along long supply chains, the ecological risks are positively correlated, meaning that if the risks to one supply chain increase, so do the risks to others (for example, if a wetland is damaged, pollination suffers in neighbouring farms). Companies importing primary products from wetlands and farms share those risks in their profit and loss accounts. That tells us that even when importing companies compete in the product market, they have an incentive to cooperate by reducing the risks they face in their supply chains. Companies have a natural incentive to cooperate in protecting ecosystems upstream in their supply chains. Investment in Nature would be the needed form of insurance.

There are ethical investors who believe that maintaining the integrity of ecosystems in their supply chains is sound business practice for companies, if for no other reason than that firms would enhance their reputation among investors. There is, of course, the risk that a company which makes a unilateral move toward ecological stewardship faces additional risks should consumers not be ecologically minded – first movers don't necessarily have an advantage. There have, however, been examples where companies have enjoyed early move advantages by declaring their trade practices to be fair. It is hard to generalise from these experiences, though. How strongly investors and consumers feel about ethical practices matters.

One way out of their dilemma would be for companies to disclose conditions in their supply chains collectively. That way the public won't need to know market prices to identify resource scarcities. In other words, disclosure could substitute for missing markets. A way to do that would be to lobby the government. Importing firms have a good reason to cooperate and insist that governments take this step. That they do not may simply reflect that the ecological basis of production chains has not yet entered business practice.

Nudging Behavioural Change

Institutional changes are one way to alter individual behaviour. Another way is to build on an insight of the behavioural psychologists Amos Tversky and Daniel Kahneman that our choices can be influenced by the way available options are framed; for example, presenting menus of choices with default options has been found to affect choices (thus affecting the quantity of provisioning goods that the global economy draws on to produce GDP). This is called 'nudging'.

Nudging was deployed in an experiment in Europe in

which opting for green household energy was made the default. Sixty-nine per cent of people in a trial of approximately 40,000 households chose the default option, compared to only 7 per cent when the supply of green energy was not the default option. Relatedly, hotels today routinely offer guests the default option of not having their bathroom towels changed.

Expanding the available set of choices by including seemingly irrelevant ones can also affect choice. In separate experiments, when more healthy options and more vegetarian meals were available in cafeterias, calorie intake and meat consumption were both reduced, despite meat and less healthy options still being available. Changing available portion sizes also has an impact. One study found that when cafeteria portion sizes were reduced, calorie intake decreased significantly, but overall satisfaction with the meal remained much the same.

There is evidence that making people associate choices with other things can alter the attractiveness of the options. Using symbols or images can make people more (or less) likely to choose an option, the association (via packaging) of cigarettes with lung disease being a powerful example. The positive effect of negative images has also been observed with unhealthy food, which is why it has been argued that more people could be pushed towards sustainable consumption through labelling the environmental harms associated with a product rather than the benefits a product is responsible for. The role of governments in bringing about these changes is obvious.

The Population Consumption Nexus

Perhaps the most sensitive issues in public policy are in connection to population and living standards. We are enjoying the historically high standard of living that is today's global per capita GDP (a bit under 20,000 international dollars) in substantial measure by not paying for the natural capital we use. If natural capital were costed at accounting prices, per capita GDP would be a lot lower. If we are resistant to any move that lowers our standard of living, it could be because we do not appreciate the provisioning goods that enter the products we consume. Bad accounting practices can distort our wants and needs.

In Chapter 6 we saw that, excepting for sub-Saharan Africa, all regions of the world have undergone a fertility transition to a TFR of less than 2.1. In the Far East and the West, TFR is now so far below this figure that the global population will reach a peak in the mid-2060s and begin to decline, even if slowly. This projection has given rise to a new worry among economic commentators, that sooner or later every big economy will hit a demographic wall and face gigantic bills from pensions and hospitals as their age distributions tilt toward the aged. Fewer young people will mean lower output and slower rates of technological progress. 'Sapped of workers and ideas,' they worry, 'economic growth could collapse while public debt balloons.'* This perspective, common today, speaks to the importance, indeed to

---

* 'Free Exchange: the old world', *The Economist* (25 May 2024), p. 73.

the necessity, of keeping global per capita GDP from ever falling – but the only way that can be achieved is by ensuring that population does not decline.

There are several flaws in this argument. One is that an aging population does not necessarily correspond to an unproductive population. Advances in medicine and health-care have meant that yesterday's 50-year-olds are today's 60-year-olds. There is no reason why the retirement age should remain frozen. It has been suggested, for example, that the retirement age should be pegged to the gap in years that existed between retirement and life expectancy at retire-ment age when the latter was drawn decades ago.

The other, and from the perspective of the Impact Inequality more serious, weakness is that the requirement that per capita GDP must not decline pays no heed to the limits of the biosphere. And it shows, once again, that our contemporary economic language does not admit to Nature setting any limits on what the human enterprise can achieve. The solution to our global ecological overreach – that we should pay for what we use – would lower our demand for Nature's provisioning goods. Today, the solution may be pol-itically unacceptable even in rich countries, but only because natural capital is absent in economic discourses.

Restoring Nature

Restoration involves helping Nature recover from a degraded, damaged, even dilapidated state. It regenerates Nature. In the language of the Impact Inequality, it is a way to increase the biosphere's combined regeneration rates.[*] Regenerated ecosystems are more effective at providing maintenance and regulating services, which have been lost in many places due to overharvesting of provisioning goods. A large-scale comparative analysis of more than 130 studies of natural regeneration in tropical forests showed that natural regeneration – that is, leaving Nature alone rather than investing labour and material to restore her – provided a benefit–cost ratio of above 4, a large figure by conventional investment standards.

Natural regeneration is often called a 'Nature-based solution', as opposed to a technological solution. Coastal defence, for example, can be achieved by restoring or creating biodiverse mudflats and sandbanks, or by the technological solution of building seawalls. There is potential for conflict between them. Moreover, technological solutions often have unanticipated, adverse effects on ecosystems. Tree planting to address climate change, for example, has frequently been interpreted too broadly, involving planting non-native tree species in areas far removed from the rainforests that were deprived, and therefore not compensating for loss of that forest's store of carbon.

Examples of Nature-based solutions now abound. Seoul, Republic of Korea, undertook an ambitious plan to restore the Cheonggyecheon River, which runs from east to west through the city. The area around the river was densely populated, and the river had become highly polluted, endangering public health. In the late 1950s, it was covered with

* That's the right-hand side of the Impact Inequality.

a four-lane road, which became a source of air pollution for the local population, who were twice as likely as people living elsewhere to suffer from respiratory diseases. The river restoration project removed the highway to uncover the river and created a 5.4km-long section consisting of terraces with plants and water channels for wildlife to thrive. Today around 20 million people visit each year. The restoration provides many benefits to the inhabitants of Seoul, including flood protection, reduced urban heat-island effect, space for recreation and recuperation, tourism, reduced particulate pollution, and areas for wildlife and biodiversity. Species richness along the restored river increased enormously in the brief period of 2003–8.

We tend to think of environmental problems in the large. The dominance of global climate change in environmental

Cheonggycheon River restoration, Seoul (Getty Images)

thinking has contributed to that, to an extent that we are led to think that 'climate' is separate from 'Nature'. But Nature is all-encompassing – climate regulation is only one among the multitude of Nature's maintenance and regulating services. What should give us hope is that Nature is most effectively restored by nurturing her in our own neighbourhood – our backyards, so to speak. Each neighbourhood is no doubt tiny, but the totality of neighbourhoods covers a good deal of Earth, some 15 per cent or thereabouts.

Climate change is a remote, seemingly abstract problem, whereas biodiversity loss is often local and tangible. The latter can even feel personal, and something over which each of us can feel we have some agency. If we appreciate the abundance that Nature offers us, and that by making changes in our personal lives we can make our habitat more liveable, we will have gone some way to restoring our place in the world around us.

CHAPTER 10

The Value of the World Around Us

The early eighteenth-century poet Alexander Pope helped popularise the modern idea that the proper study of 'Mankind' is man. I don't know whether Pope intended to interpret 'man' narrowly, but one strand of Enlightenment thinking, perhaps all Enlightenment thinking, sees the human person as above Nature, a supreme creature, in beauty and intellect. That picture has filtered down to our daily cultural life, at least in the West, with its celebration of ourselves, where human achievement is seen standing outside all else. It directs us to measure Nature in terms of her use value and her amenity value to us.

But there are times when that is not enough for us. In those moments, we want to break out of that perception and value Nature because she is sacred to us, even that she has moral standing. From time to time, these thoughts come to us effortlessly. When we experience the teeming life of a tropical wetland and the sounds and movements of its insects, birds and plants there, it is hard for us to accept that Nature has no purpose – that her processes, mostly silent and invisible, are blind forces at work in creating the complex environment of which we are a part. But *we* have purpose, and it is that which gives our lives grace and moves us to imagine that Nature has a purpose. In doing so, we are persuaded she has an *intrinsic value*. And once we acknowledge that, we begin to doubt whether hard-nosed cost–benefit analysis could be the right language to express our relationship to her.

Aspects of Nature demand care and consideration in other ways. Many people, perhaps in all societies, locate the sacred in her. And the sacred is not negotiable unless we rationalise by imagining it to be incorruptible. The Ganges is a mother goddess to Hindus; she is *Ma Ganga*. Yet, she is one of the most polluted rivers in the world. It is said that being celestial, the Ganges cannot be corrupted, that the pollution we see being carried in her waters is itself a form of cleansing. We compromise and we rationalise.

In Benin, legislation has enshrined the sanctity of sacred groves into law. The country has nearly 3,000 tiny sacred groves – some 70 per cent are less than a hectare in extent. Many social practices of communities there rely on materials and resources drawn directly from forests: leaves, animals, water and stones. But hunting is prohibited, as is setting fires in the groves.

Forests are, however, disappearing in Benin. In 1990, they covered over 40 per cent of land; today, due to agricultural extensions, hunting, grazing and timber extraction, the figure is less than 30 per cent. In 2012, the Benin government introduced a decree that gave legal recognition to sacred forests as protected areas. It protects the areas through local management, by integrating traditional custodians and community authorities.

Many today would regard an awareness of the sacred to

encompass a sense of awe and wonder, of self-transcendence, through which we locate ourselves within the landscape around us and imagine what lies beyond. That sense is not confined to what are often called 'traditional cultures'. Many of the creation hymns and invocations to the Supreme Being by the poet Rabindranath Tagore have roots in the Vedanta,* but they are detached from the rituals that had been given expression in Vedic times. They invoke the transcendent, but they are not tied to organised religion.

The historian Simon Schama has argued that it is a mistake to think that Western cultures have abandoned the spiritual aspects of Nature, that they have left behind the myths that were created round her. He has shown that the transcendent has been expressed repeatedly in art and architecture. And that sense of spirituality is often experienced today not in isolation, but communally, such as among birdwatchers, hikers, cyclists, surfers, divers and anglers.

The sense of transcendence that Nature invokes may exist everywhere, but it has taken a severe beating in modern times. Our contending needs and wants together have blunted our feeling that by protecting the landscape we protect ourselves. The ability of rich societies to desecrate the landscape elsewhere has helped to accommodate those conflicting feelings, and the discipline of economics has increasingly aided that accommodation. Economic justification in rich countries is all too often a euphemism for commercial justification, and in poor countries the term

---

* The Vedanta are the conclusion of the Vedas, the oldest scriptures in Hinduism, originating in the second millennium BCE.

'economic development' is routinely used to justify appall-
ing investment undertakings.

That need not have been. Correct economic reasoning is
grounded on our values. These values are sharpened when
we recognise our embeddedness in Nature. To detach Nature
from economics is to imply that we consider ourselves to be
external to her. The fault is not in economics; it lies in the
way we have chosen to practise it.

Nature's Moral Standing

The sacredness of Nature points to an existence value, and
even the intrinsic worth that we have discussed so far is a
value *we* impart to her. But does Nature also have moral
standing independent of us? Hindu ethics attributes rights
to Nature. In contrast, the UK Environmental Law Association (UKELA) has published studies that face the question
from a legal point of view. They have proposed 'wild law' and
'earth jurisprudence', concepts that give legal standing to non-
human parts of the biosphere, such as plants, animals and
even ecosystems. These ideas go beyond traditional notions of
conservation – in which Nature is protected because humans
want it to be – by providing legal rights and interests to Nature
so that it can be represented in the courts of law. In a 2009
study, the UKELA found instances of wild law in many countries around the world, including New Zealand, India, Ecuador,
the United States and Colombia. These legal terms are clearly
founded on moral thinking about the nature and value of ecosystems but are primarily concerned with legal processes.

To assess whether ecosystems have moral standing, it is useful to start by comparing them with the entity most universally accepted as being morally significant: ourselves. The notion of personhood provides the basis of our moral standing. One prominent conception has it that personhood is an innate and intrinsic property of all humans. The question as to whether it is appropriate to impart a notion of personhood to ecosystems is thus a question about whether there is some aspect of these systems that is at least partially analogous to the quality of personhood possessed by human beings, and is thus worthy of our moral respect.

A key aspect of personhood is identifying a self. Normally this self is identified by the limits of the human body and the span of our lives. But the definition is problematic. Our teeth, for instance, are a part of us and have moral importance in being so. Should they become detached (as children's teeth naturally do) they would seem to lose some, but perhaps not all, of this significance. Many of us are also now intimately bound up with technologies that we also incorporate into ourselves, from artificial heart valves to robotic arms, and we even extend the self in some respects to cover personal property, especially where this has more than monetary value to the person who possesses it. And, of course, our bodies are not, in fact, just one organism, but an entire microbiome in which non-human cells (on our skin, in our guts and just about everywhere in between) outnumber the human cells by quite a margin.

It is natural for us to adopt a notion of ourselves that is sufficiently permissive to encompass these kinds of oddities and boundary cases. However, there is an argument to be made that we significantly underestimate just how embedded our human bodies are in Nature, and that such broader notions of the self would let in far more than we realise. We may correctly judge that because none of us could digest food without the bacteria in our gut, we should treat those bacteria as part of us. But if we do that, why should we not just as equally judge that because we could not breathe without the plants in our garden and elsewhere, we should also treat them as being part of us? Effectively, what such an argument does is to make the case that we should internalise those ecosystem services that are essential to human survival, and not just the tiny percentage of those that take place within the confines of our bodies. This kind of argument may appear to have powerful implications for how we should treat natural ecosystems (i.e., no less favourably than we would ourselves), but ultimately what it leaves us with is the humans we began with, only this time these persons are understood to overlap and extend to cover the entire biosphere they inhabit.

And yet, and yet . . . All this reasoning is far too cold for our comfort. Intellectualising our place in Nature misses something of supreme importance; the emotional attachment to her that we feel we are in danger of tearing apart. Many, perhaps most, of Nature's processes are silent and invisible. I have used those two features to understand how we have allowed ourselves in the Anthropocene to undermine Nature so extensively, that we are at risk of overwhelming ourselves. The two features also tell us that neither the law nor the force of social norms of behaviour can ultimately make us protect Nature from ourselves. What remains is self-monitoring of personal conduct, the realisation that we are part of Nature. Ultimately, we must be our own judge and jury if we are to protect ourselves.

How can we do this? How can we create the incentives to behave? It seems to me it is only possible if we develop a love for Nature. For if you love a being, you will want to protect her. And we can develop a love for Nature only if we develop an understanding of her processes, to appreciate the rhythms of the bewildering range and reach she displays. And the only way to catch a glimpse of that is through education.

We live in a world that is increasingly urban – nearly 60 per cent of the global population live in towns or cities. Many children today have no conception of Nature's workings beneath their feet, nor do they see much green in their neighbourhoods. One way to bring their lives closer to our roots is to transform our education curricula to include Nature studies from the earliest years of schooling, carrying on as a matter of course through the latter years of formal education. It is only when we begin to appreciate beauty in what we otherwise see as muck in marshes and woodlands that we develop a sense of wonder at Nature's processes. That is also when we begin to appreciate her abundance, perhaps even her sacredness.

The Repugnance of Human Extinction

Runaway carbon emissions and biodiversity loss are interfering so much with the workings of the biosphere that humanity now faces a problem it did not face in the past:

a human-created possibility of our collective extinction. Death is inevitable for every person. While each death is a loss, we mostly accept its inevitability. The possibility of human extinction, in contrast, is so alien to our sensibilities that we do not yet have an accepted vocabulary in which to deliberate it. We realise that the loss would be all the lives that could have existed but would now not be lived; the unsettled vocabulary concerns the way we should evaluate that loss.

Risks of extinction, such as the kind of event that led to the fifth extinction some 66 million years ago (known as *exogenous risks*), are probabilistically inevitable; we are not responsible for them. In contrast, we *would* be responsible for the risks of extinction that would be avoided if only we were to change our behaviour. That is why extinction risks that our actions give rise to have greater moral gravity than those over which we have no control. Climate change and biodiversity loss, which both heighten the risk of extinction, are two such examples. Emitting even a billion tons of carbon into the atmosphere today raises the risk of extinction, even if ever so slightly, and the rate at which our activities are causing species to become extinct adds to that risk.

But there is something cold and impersonal about assessing the moral gravity of human extinction in terms of the loss of wellbeing of all who would then not exist. We feel we need a reason closer to home, one that speaks to our emotions. In *The Fate of the Earth*, his deep meditation on the significance of a possible nuclear holocaust, the writer Jonathan Schell described the dilemma thus:

It is of the essence of the human condition that we are born, live for a while, and then die . . . But although the untimely death of everyone in the world would in itself be an unimaginably huge loss, it would bring with it a separate, distinct loss that would be in a sense even huger – the cancellation of all future generations of human beings. (Schell, 1982: 114–15)

Schell's book was originally published as a three-part essay in the *New Yorker* in 1981, at the height of the Cold War. Schell was a writer, not a professional philosopher, but he made not one false move in philosophical reasoning in the crucial middle chapter, 'Second Death'. Utilitarianism measures the loss from the Second Death in terms of the wellbeing of all who would not exist on account of human extinction. Schell, however, made a different move, which could be read as internalising wellbeing across the generations. He wrote of the loss each of us alive today would suffer if we were to discover that there will be no one after we are gone, and he attributed the loss *not* to any attachment that we may have to humanity writ large, but to a devaluation of our own lives. And he used the artist and his art to make the point:

There is no doubt that art, which breaks into the crusted and hardened patterns of thought and feeling in the present as though it were the prow of the future, is in radically altered circumstances if the future is placed in doubt. The ground on which the artist stands when he turns to his work has grown unsteady beneath his feet. (Schell, 1982: 163)

Schell spoke of the artist, but he could have made the same case for all who create ideas and objects. Future people add value to the creators' lives by making their creations durable. An artist may regard his work to be far more important than parenting, but he is helped by the presumption that there will be future generations to bestow durability upon it.

The examples Schell pointed to were works of art and discoveries in the sciences. Those creations are public goods, but most of us don't have the talent to produce them. Confining attention to public goods is not only limiting, but it also raises an ethical dilemma: suppose we were all indifferent to having children and stared only at the prospective costs of raising them. We would free ride our responsibility to help repopulate the world by having none, and the artist would be mistaken in his assumption that there will be future people to give durability to his work.

Nevertheless, the direction Schell was pointing to is exactly right. Public goods aren't the only objects of ethical significance. Our values and practices are significant too. Many are private, even confined to the family, and it is important to us that they are passed down to our children, and by them to their children, into an indefinite future. Procreation is a means of making our values and practices durable. We imbue our children with values we cherish and teach them the practices we believe are right not merely because we think it is good for them, but also because we desire to see our values and practices survive.

Those values and practices are not public goods. On the

contrary, we cherish them *because* they are intimate. They are stories we tell our children of our own joys, sorrows and discomfiture, of their grandparents' foibles, and we instruct them on the family rituals we ourselves inherited from our parents. We may have modified the rituals, but we didn't invent them from scratch. Our descendants do something supremely important for us: they add value to our lives that our own mortality would otherwise deprive them of.

The springs that motivate humankind to assume parenthood are deep and abiding. Their genetic basis explains the motivation but doesn't justify it. Justification is to be found elsewhere. Our children provide us with a means of self-transcendence, the widest avenue open to us of living *through* time, not merely *in* time. Mortality threatens to render the achievements of our life as transitory, and this threat is removed by procreation. The ability to leave descendants enables us to invest in projects that will not cease to have value once we are gone, projects that justify life rather than merely serve it. Not all have held this view. Alexander Herzen's famous remark, that human development is a kind of chronological unfairness because those who live later profit from the labour of their predecessors without paying the same price, reflects an extreme form of alienation, as does Kant's anxiety that earlier generations should carry their burdens only for the sake of the later ones, that only the last should have the good fortune to dwell in the completed building. As they saw it, we can do something for posterity, but it can do nothing for us. This, as we have seen, is a deep misconception.

The motivation we are identifying here transmutes

from the individual to the collective. Every generation is a trustee of a wide range of assets, be they cultural or moral, produced or natural, it has inherited from the past. Looking backward, it acknowledges an implicit understanding with the previous generation of receiving the capital in return for its transmission, modified suitably in the light of changing circumstances and increasing knowledge. Looking forward, it offers an implicit proposal to the next generation of bequeathing its stocks of assets, that they in turn may be modified suitably by it and then passed on to the following generation. This perspective is not at odds with the conception of wellbeing across the generations. In our account of ethics in a world moving through time, each generation would be moved to internalise the potential wellbeing of its descendants. Our descendants are not us, but they are not outside us either.

Schell's reflections point also to the intrinsic value of Nature. It's a mistake to seek justification for the preservation of ecological diversity, or more narrowly the protection of species, solely on instrumental grounds; that is on grounds that we know they are useful to us or may prove useful to our descendants. As we have seen, such arguments have a role, but they are not sufficient. Nor can the argument rely on the welfare of the members of such species (it does not account for the special role that species preservation plays in the argument), or on the 'rights' of animals. A full justification bases itself as well on how we see ourselves, on what our informed desires are. In examining our values and thus our lives, we are led to ask whether the destruction of an entire species-habitat for some immediate gratification is something that we can live with comfortably. The idea of intergenerational exchange is embedded in the perspective of eternity, but the mistake is to see ecological preservation as matters of personal and political morality. They are at least as much a matter of personal and political ethics.

Glossary

Accounting prices – the social weights that economists attach to the demands we make of all categories of provisioning goods (those that we harvest or extract from ecosystems, such as food and freshwater). Formally, the accounting price of a good or service is the contribution that an additional unit of it would make to social wellbeing, other things remaining the same.

Anthropocene – an unofficial geological epoch (marked by the appearance of large deposits of metals, pesticides, concrete, nitrogen, plastics, phosphorus and aluminium, as well as concentrations of carbon dioxide and methane, in the soil, seabed and water) beginning in the mid-twentieth century, highlighting a sharp rise in human activities and the fact that we are now living in a human-dominated planet.

Assets – goods that are assigned with a positive value; economists call them 'capital assets' or 'capital goods'.

Biodiversity – the diversity of species and the genes that combine to form the organisms that comprise the species, but also the diversity of and within ecosystems. Biodiversity increases an ecosystem's resilience to shocks and reduces risks to the goods and services it produces.

Biomass – renewable organic material from plants and animals, which can be measured in quantity (for example, the biomass in a forest).

Biosphere – used throughout this book as a more specific version of Nature, it is commonly used to refer to the areas of Earth where there are living things, the global sum of all ecosystems.

Capital assets/goods – the term assigned by economists to assets, and which today includes knowledge (as in 'knowledge capital'); the law, government, the market system and financial institutions (as in 'institutional capital'); mutual trust, social norms and group solidarity (as in 'social capital'); culture and personal norms, and the rituals that go with them (as in 'cultural capital'); and even religion (as in 'religious capital').

Common property resources (CPRs) – communitarian systems of governance that are neither private nor state property but are also not open access. They are communal property, involving tight adherence to social norms, and anthropologists, economists and political scientists have uncovered numerous examples, including village ponds, woodlands, marshes, coastal fisheries, meadows, grazing fields, mangrove forests and water holes.

Conservation – the protection of Nature, traditionally anthropocentric and driven by human ends. More recent ideas go beyond this, suggesting that Nature should be provided with legal rights and interests so that it can be represented in the courts of law. There are now instances of 'wild law' in many countries around the world.

Cultural services – the non-material benefits provided by ecosystems, including spiritual experiences and an identification with religious values. People find aesthetic value in Nature, which finds expression in private gardens, public parks and protected areas. Ecosystems influence social relationships and local ecosystems offer people a sense of place, a cultural landscape.

Ecological footprint – the quantity of provisioning goods drawn from the biosphere in a period. What is drawn is mostly visible and recordable. It is the society's direct demands from Nature in a period. The corresponding indirect demands – we can call them 'needs' – are for Nature's maintenance and regulating services. Humanity would be overreaching for provisioning goods if the global ecological footprint exceeded the biosphere's regeneration rate, that is, the regeneration rate of provisioning goods.

Economic model – a simplified description of reality, which can be used by economists to create hypotheses about economic behaviour which can then be tested. Nature has frequently been excluded from such models.

Ecosystem – a complex of living organisms (plants, animals, fungi and microorganisms) and their non-living environment in a particular location that together combine to control such natural processes as energy flow and material recycling. Ecosystems can overlap and blend into one another, with varying degrees of interaction among their own constituents and across boundaries. They also vary in their spatial reach, from the Amazon rainforest down to the collection of micro-organisms occupying the gut of an animal.

Ecosystem function – the biological, geochemical and physical processes that occur within an ecosystem (for example, nutrient cycling).

Ecosystem services – the positive benefits that ecosystems provide to people, ranging from provisioning goods such as food, water and timber, to regulating services that affect climate and disease, to cultural services such as recreational spiritual benefits, and maintenance services such as soil formation.

Enabling assets – an economy's intangible infrastructure that enables the global economy to deploy produced capital, human capital and natural capital for our purposes; for example, the legal system and social customs have increased the quantity of provisioning goods that the global economy draws upon to produce GDP.

Eukaryote – organisms with cells containing a distinct nucleus that houses genetic material in the form of chromosomes. This covers everything with membrane-bound nuclei from a single-cell organism to the blue whale.

Externalities – unaccounted-for consequences for others of events for which we are responsible. The qualifier 'unaccounted-for' means that the consequences in question follow without prior engagement with those who are affected. As the externalities we are considering throughout the book are transmitted through the material world, we call them 'environmental externalities'. They can be negative – for example, the damage caused by phosphorus compounds leaking from farms and finding their way into rivers – or positive – for example, the beneficial externalities conferred on people downstream by upstream farmers when they plant trees on their land to reduce soil erosion.

Gross domestic product (GDP) – the market value of the flow of all final goods and services produced within a country in a year. It includes the market value of aggregate private consumption, or consumer spending, gross investment (including the capital expenditures of businesses), the sum of government expenditures, and the difference between exports and imports. GDP is a measure of an economy's aggregate output.

Gross national income (GNI) – total income earned by residents of a given country, both domestically and internationally regardless of location, minus income paid to non-residents in a period.

Holocene – the present geological epoch, beginning some 12,000 years ago after the Last Glacial Period (the latest 'Ice Age').

Human capital – intangible assets (such as health, education, aptitude) and ideas (science and technology).

Impact Inequality – a measure of global ecological overreach. If global population multiplied by global per capita GDP (Ny), divided by the efficiency with which provisioning goods are drawn upon to produce GDP (α), exceeds the biosphere's combined regeneration rate (G), then it can be said that there is global ecological overreach.

Inclusive wealth – the accounting value of an economy's assets, to include the value of natural capital.

International dollars – a hypothetical unit of currency that has the same purchasing power as the US dollar in the United States at a point in time.

Market price – the price that something can be sold for at a point in time.

Microbiome – the community of microorganisms found together in a particular environment, such as the human body.

Natural capital – the world's stock of natural resources, including not only living organisms, but also materials and non-living organisms, such as sand, gravel and detritus.

Natural resources – the material resources that are drawn directly from Nature.

Open access resources – non-alienable, non-excludable assets, free to all who want to make use of them, such as the atmosphere and the high seas.

Option value – the additional value derived from keeping options open through, for example, the conservation of certain species whose role in the health of an ecosystem may not yet be fully understood. This value is a good reason for giving populations of species a wider berth.

Primary producers – photosynthesising organisms at the bottom of the food chain.

Produced capital – physical, tangible assets such as roads, ports, buildings and machines.

Protected area – a clearly defined geographical space, such as a national park or nature reserve, which is set aside through legal or other means in order to achieve certain conservation objectives.

Public goods – assets that are non-excludable and non-rivalrous (use by a person or a group of persons does not diminish the asset's availability to others). Examples include the climate, a field of study like calculus, or a piece of knowledge such as the formula for a manufacturing process.

Regeneration rate (of an ecosystem) – the ability of an ecosystem to bounce back and recover from damage. The biosphere's regeneration rate is the rate at which provisioning goods recover.

Replacement (fertility) rate – an approximation of the total fertility rate (TFR) at which population, in time, would be constant; calculated, correcting for early mortality, to be 2.1.

Restoration – involves helping Nature recover from a degraded, damaged, even dilapidated state. It regenerates Nature. In the language of the Impact Inequality, it is a way to increase the biosphere's combined regeneration rates.

Social capital – mutual trust, social norms and group solidarity, which allow for a society to function effectively.

Social cost–benefit analysis – a comparison of the gains and losses in society's welfare that follow a specific project or policy.

Species – a population whose members can interbreed freely under 'natural conditions'; the lowest rung in the hierarchical classification of life forms, which runs as species, genus, family, order, class, phylum and kingdom. Each rung higher than that of species is a cluster of species that resemble one another and are thought to share a common ancestry.

Sustainable development – development that meets the needs of the present without compromising the ability of future generations to meet their own needs, as defined by the Brundtland Report in 1987. The Brundtland criterion asks us to compare economic opportunities at different points in time and defines sustainable development to be paths along which those opportunities expand continually (or, more accurately, don't ever contract). Because we shouldn't expect there to be a unique sustainable development path – the criterion does not distinguish the composition of capital assets on the many potential paths along which opportunities expand continually – we would need additional criteria to be able to choose among them. The Brundtland criterion can thus be thought of as a basic requirement, nothing more.

Sustainable Development Goals (SDGs) – adopted by member countries of the United Nations in 2015 as their vison for the future to be attained by 2030. They range from zero global poverty (Goal 1) to collective action among nations to bring about the goals (Goal 17).

Tipping point (ecological) – the critical threshold at which an ecosystem's health is seriously compromised to the point that further pressure will result in a new state of ecological balance that is potentially irreversible. Fig. 1*.1 includes a range of examples, such as clear-water lakes becoming turbid-water lakes, coral-dominated reefs switching to algae-dominated reefs, and grassland shifting to shrub-bushland.

Total fertility rate (TFR) – the number of times on average a woman gives birth over her reproductive years, taken to be 15–49.

Utilitarianism – an ethical theory in which social wellbeing is judged to be a weighted sum of individual wellbeings, the weights reflecting the trade-offs among different people's wellbeing that we think are permissible when we deliberate over alternative economic paths.

Watershed – an area of land that divides waters flowing to different waterbodies.

Notes and Further Reading

CHAPTER I: NATURE IS AN ASSET

The text spoke of multiple tipping points in ecosystem processes. Fig. 1*.1 (figures within this Notes and Further Reading section, rather than the main chapters, are marked with an asterisk), taken from Folke et al. (2004), gives an illustration of tipping points in a wide range of familiar ecosystems.

FIG 1*.1 MULTIPLE STABILITY REGIMES

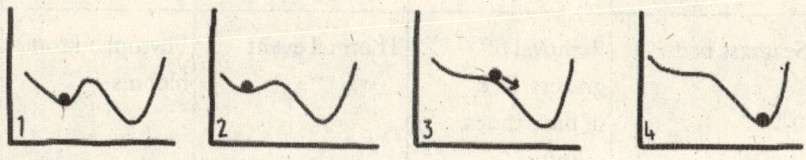

SOURCE : FOLK ET AL. (2004)

GRAPH 1	GRAPH 2	GRAPH 3	GRAPH 4
Clear-water lakes	Phosphorous accumulation in agricultural soil and lake mud	Flooding, warming, overexploitation of predators	Turbid-water lakes

Coral-dominated reefs	Overfishing, coastal eutrophication	Diseases, bleaching hurricane	Algae-dominated reefs
Grassland	Fire prevention	Good rains, continuous heavy grazing	Shrub-bushland
Grassland	Hunting of herbivores	Disease	Woodland
Kelp forests	Functional elimination of apex predators	Thermal event, storm, disease	Sea urchin dominance
Pine forest	Microclimate and soil changes, loss of pine regeneration	Decreased fire frequency, increased fire intensity	Oak forest
Seagrass beds	Removal of grazers, lack of hurricanes, salinity moderation, spatial homogenization	Thermal event	Phytoplankton blooms
Tropical lake with submerged vegetation	Nutrient accumulation during dry spells	Nutrient release with water table rise	Floating-plant dominance

A pioneering case-study on the protection that mangrove forests provide for coastal populations is Das and Vincent (2009). On synchronisation among connected oscillating systems, see Strogatz (2003), and the more technical rendering in Pikovsky, Rosenblum and Kurths

(2001). To obtain an expert sense of the connections between biodiversity loss and global climate change, see the collection of essays in Lovejoy and Hannah (2019). There are many textbooks and readers in ecology. Bowman and Hacker (2023) is an excellent introduction. Levin (2009) remains the outstanding collection of essays on key ideas in the subject. But to get an emotional feel for ecology, one cannot do better than to read Carson (1951), the marine biologist Rachel Carson's meditation on the oceans. Using fungi as the object for understanding the silence of Nature's processes, Sheldrake (2020) is a modern masterpiece of scientific writing.

The environmentalist James Lovelock was the first to read Earth as a self-regulating system possessing stability within bounds, like a living organism. He called that reading the Gaia Hypothesis (Lovelock, 1979). Initially subjected to ridicule by prominent evolutionary biologists, developments in the mathematics of complex systems have given substance to Lovelock's colourful, if somewhat anthropocentric, christening of the processes governing the Earth system.

CHAPTER 2: HOW BIODIVERSITY WORKS

Species-area relationships were formulated as equilibrium conditions in MacArthur and Wilson (1967). The authors studied biodiversity in islands of differing size. Durrett and Levin (1996) studied processes that yield species-area curves as equilibrium conditions. Rosenzweig (1995) provides an excellent account of species diversity in both space and time. For review of what we know about the number of species today, see Mora et al. (2011). On species extinctions, see Ehrlich, Ceballos and Dirzo (2024). A classic on the content and significance of biodiversity is Wilson (1992). On functional biodiversity and ecosystem productivity, see Tilman and Downing (1994) and Tilman et al. (2014). Levin (2001, with a new edition in 2017) is a multi-volume encyclopaedia of ecology in which readers will find reviews of every topic of special interest to them.

CHAPTER 3: HUMAN IMPACT IN THE PAST

A powerful study of the ways in which the biosphere has been shaped by co-evolution of we humans and other species is Ehrlich and Ehrlich (2008). The authors track the emergence of humans as the dominant species. Scholes and Walker (1993) is a study of the ways in which the African Savanna has been (and is being) shaped by human population. Barbier (2011) explores the ways human groups everywhere and always have deployed natural resources to meet their needs. The author pays especial attention to the links between resource use and the character of economic development. Frankopan (2023) is a monumental study of the influence of the local environment on the character of societies and the influence of human societies on the biosphere.

A highly original study of what one could call the geographical history of societies is Diamond (1997). The puzzle Diamond poses is why Eurasia (including Egypt because of its near contiguity to Eurasia) was until the modern era the seat of the world's economic centres, alternating within its ends, and not Africa or the Americas. His answer is that Eurasia ranges east–west in a temperate clime, offering broad climatic similarities. Not blocked by mountain ranges, there were passable routes in the land mass along which goods (e.g., seeds) and ideas could travel. The famous Silk Roads were an example. Centres flourished alternatingly, but civilisation did not die in the continent. In contrast, or so Diamond argued, the Americas have a north–south alignment, as does Africa. There are rich details Diamond goes into, but his central point is that ecological disparities within each of the latter two continental masses were too great for goods, people and ideas to travel back and forth easily. A further feature, or so Diamond points to, was the presence of domesticable animals; wild horses and cattle in Eurasia, in contrast to Africa, which was home to zebras and, in many places, the tsetse fly.

On the dominance of Europe from the Early Modern period (1500 CE), there are many books and articles, but for me Landes (1998) is the defining investigation. In a characteristically bold and original work, the physicist Steven Weinberg (2016) has argued that the sixteenth to seventeenth centuries were not simply the period of the Scientific Revolution, but more significantly were when modern science – that is, science as it is practised today – was discovered.

CHAPTER 4: THE IMPACT INEQUALITY

Micklethwait and Wooldridge (2003) and Ridley (2010) are only two of an enormous list of publications that extol the achievement of the human economy in the post-war period, while avoiding mention of the costs we have been silently incurring as we further cripple the biosphere. Ehrlich and Ehrlich (1981) is a classic work on the extinction of species – it brought the subject to the public. Dasgupta, Raven and McIvor (2019) is a collection of essays on the general phenomenon of biological extinctions. Ehrlich, Ceballos and Dirzo (2024) is a book-length review of what we know today about species extinction rates. Figures for the state of the oceans have been taken from Sullivan et al. (2019). On anthropogenic sources of the ongoing climate change today, the latest report by IPCC (2023) offers a comprehensive account. For proposals on what we should do about it, see Barrett (2003, 2012) and Stern (2015). Haque et al. (2022) is a collection of field studies on ways communities in South Asia have adapted in recent years to cope with the increased variability of the climate.

The book that brought home to the public the dire effects on insects of industrial chemicals is Carson (1962). For years now, it has been the bible of the environmental movement in the West. But chemical companies spent millions attempting to counter the science and evidence Carson had used in her book.

The term human 'impact' for what we today call 'ecological footprint' was introduced by Ehrlich and Holdren (1971). Barrett, Dasgupta, Dasgupta et al. (2019) deployed it in their formulation of the idea of ecological overreach and called it the 'Impact Inequality'. It formed an essential building block in Dasgupta (2021, [2024]), which explores the wide-ranging implications of viewing economic possibilities in terms of our place in Nature. On forest fragmentation and the disproportionate loss in biological productivity resulting from it, see Laurance et al. (2002) and Siegel et al. (2024). Formal models of macro-economic possibilities in a bounded Earth are in Dasgupta (2021 [2024], Chapters 4 and 10).

IUCN's Red List identifies ecosystems that that are experiencing varying degrees of threat. The links have been also studied at the planetary level by Rockström et al. (2009). The authors, in the main Earth scientists, identified nine physical markers (planetary boundaries) of the state of the biosphere: climate regulation, novel entities, available freshwater, biospheric integrity (roughly, biodiversity), stratospheric ozone level, ocean acidity, biogeochemical flows (nitrogen and phosphorus cycles), aerosol loading in the atmosphere, and land use (e.g., forest cover). Fig. 4*.1, taken from Richardson et al. (2023), is an update of Rockström et al. (2009). The authors identify the safe operating zone for each of the nine markers and estimate their current levels, expressed in terms of the risks they pose to the biosphere's regenerative capacity. The figure shows that four of the boundaries have been breached: climate regulation, biodiversity, phosphorous and nitrogen cycles, and land use (diversity of ecosystems). The figure is consistent with the findings of reported in Chapter 4.

How Many People Can Earth Support?

The Impact Inequality leads to an irresistible question: what size of the human population can the biosphere support at a reasonable standard of living? There are commentators (e.g., *The Economist*) who insist that the world is 'not yet full', but do not provide quantitative

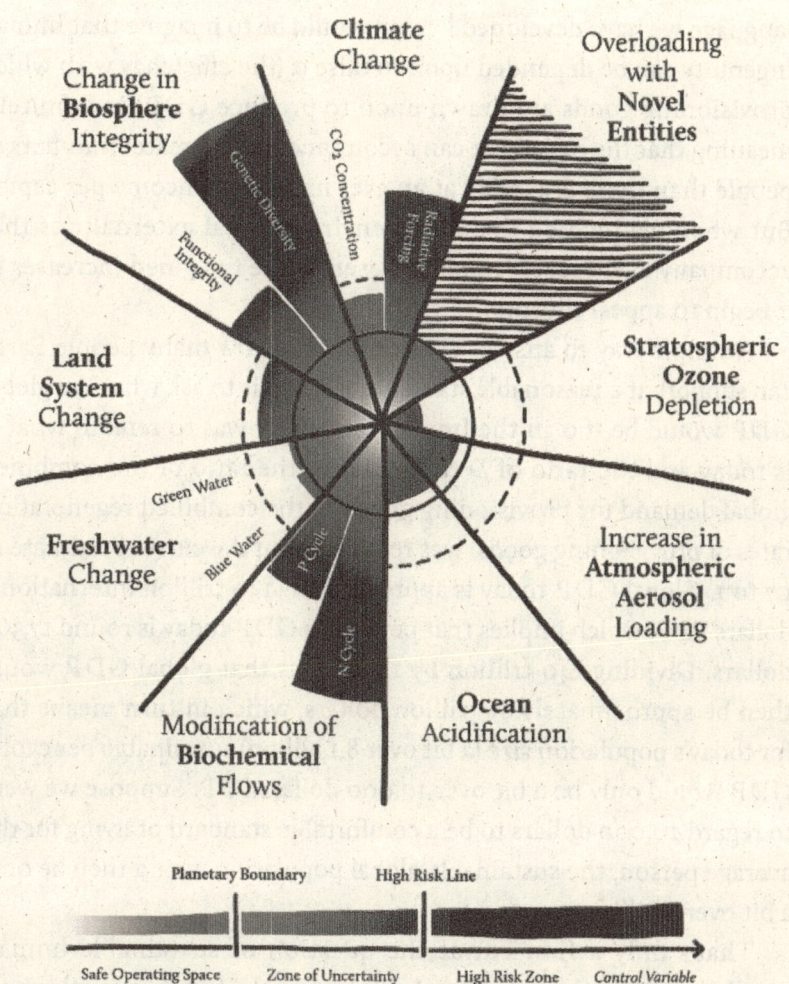

SOURCE: RICHARDSON ET AL. (2023)

evidence. Significantly, they don't include our ecological footprint in their discourse: the authors merely assert.* If we were to use the language we have developed here, it would be to imagine that human ingenuity can be depended upon to raise α (the efficiency with which provisioning goods are drawn upon to produce GDP) indefinitely, meaning that the biosphere can accommodate far greater numbers of people than there are today at an ever increasing income per capita. But when we include the added environmental externalities that accompany ever greater human presence, the imagined increases in α begin to appear illusory.

A simple way to answer the question of how many people Earth can support at a reasonable standard of living is to ask what the global GDP would be if α in the Impact Inequality was to remain what it is today and the ratio of D to G (that is, the ratio of the combined global demand for provisioning goods to the combined regeneration rates of provisioning goods) was reduced from the current estimate of 1.7 to 1. Global GDP today is approximately 140 trillion international dollars PPP, which implies that per capita GDP today is round 17,500 dollars. Dividing 140 trillion by 1.7 tells us that global GDP would then be approximately 82 trillion dollars, which in turn means that for today's population size (a bit over 8.1 billion) sustainable per capita GDP would only be a bit over 10,000 dollars PPP. Suppose we were to regard 20,000 dollars to be a comfortable standard of living for the average person, the sustainable global population would then be only a bit over 4 billion people.

That's only a first cut at the question of sustainable human population. The calculation hasn't allowed for the fact that people aren't merely consumers, they are producers too, which means that global per capita GDP, y, in the Impact Inequality is dependent on the level of the global population, N. Moreover, we haven't included the fact that children and old people don't work in the formal market. We would also have to postulate a global production function that transforms

* 'The baby-bust economy', *Economist*, 3 June 2023, p. 10.

factor inputs into global GDP. Including these features would alter the estimate. One exercise, in Dasgupta and Dasgupta (2022), deployed a familiar global production model to arrive at a figure of some 3.4 billion people. That was global population in the mid-1960s, so we are speaking of a recent past.

CHAPTER 5: THE CONSEQUENCES OF OUR ACTIONS

Natural capital is essential for our existence. We are embedded in Nature; we are not external to her. But until recently, influential writers on economic development saw natural capital mostly as luxuries. An unnecessary debate took place between those who expressed environmental concerns in relation to low-income countries and those who saw the need for economic growth there above all else. Well-meaning writers tried to reconcile the two viewpoints. An editorial in the UK's *Independent* (4 December 1999), for example, observed that economic 'growth is good for the environment because countries need to put poverty behind them in order to care', and a column in *The Economist* on the same day insisted that 'trade improves the environment, because it raises incomes, and the richer people are, the more willing they are to devote resources to cleaning up their living space'.

The origins of this misleading view can be traced to the World Bank (1992), which reported that in cross-country studies the emission of sulphur and nitrogen oxides had been found to be related to per capita GDP in the form of an inverse U. Emissions were found to increase with per capita GDP when countries are poor, but to decline with per capita GDP when countries are rich. Inevitably, the relationship was named the 'environmental Kuznets curve', in honour of the economist Simon Kuznets, who had observed an inverse-U relationship between per capita GDP and income inequality (Kuznets, 1941).

Competition for Nature's multitude of provisioning goods has been a prime force behind the way the biosphere has been transformed. Moreover, commercial demand frequently trumps local needs, especially under non-democratic regimes. International public opinion is often tepid. The complex relationships between the factors that have given rise to our ecological overreach have been ignored in growth and development economics and the economics of poverty. In the event, the economics of biodiversity was left to be developed by a few economists and ecologists working together. For a formal demonstration of the way harvesting costs affect the fate of open access resources, see Dasgupta, Mitra and Sorger (2019).

The error in believing reductions in the time-price of goods quoted in Chapter 5 are a sign of increasing abundance of natural resources is in Tupy and Pooley (2022).

The philosophical literature on personal and social wellbeing is enormous. A classic is Sidgwick (1907). The version I have adopted in the text is from Griffin (1986).

CHAPTER 6: THE INFLUENCE OF OTHERS

Douglas and Isherwood (1979) is the classic anthropological study of consumption as a social activity. Easterlin (1974) inspired studies on the idea that in societies that are not poor, it is relative income, not absolute income, that most matters for happiness and life satisfaction. Even weaker forms of the claim remain foreign in economics textbooks. Layard and De Neve (2023) is the book to read on the subject.

Socially embedded preferences are not yet part of mainstream growth and development economics nor the economics of poverty. There is a small, exceptional set of papers on the subject, exemplified in the collection of essays in Benhabib et al. (2011). Trentmann (2016) is a monumental study of the emergence and growth of modern consumption practices since the Early Modern period.

Bongaarts (2011, 2016, 2019, 2020) are essential readings on the contemporary demographic picture of sub-Saharan Africa. The issues he raises there, based on evidence drawn from the subcontinent, are avoided by development economists, national and international decision makers, development and environmental charities, and many other groups besides. I have even heard environmental activists dismissing concerns about population pressures as mere distraction.

It wasn't so previously, but in UNFPA (1995), a publication that followed the 1994 UN International Conference on Population and Development in Cairo, the language of 'rights' was enshrined in the sphere of family planning and reproductive health. Subsequent writings affirming the UN declaration have interpreted the passage and its intent narrowly, by focusing on the right to decide freely, with little consideration of *collective* responsibility. Recently, UNFPA (2023) has reinforced the viewpoint in a campaign that celebrates humanity's reaching 8 billion people in late 2022, by asserting that in asking, 'Too many people? Too few? What is the right number?', the 'world' is posing the wrong questions. The communication accuses those who ask, 'are there too many people?' as 'population alarmists', having an agenda that 'paint[s] a picture of out-of-control, unstoppable birth rates, usually pointing the finger at poor and marginalized communities'. The right question, UNFPA says, is: 'Are people, especially women, able to freely make their own reproductive choice?' But if additional births widen the Impact Inequality, why do the rights of contemporary people to reproduce trump the rights of future people to inherit a healthy biosphere? The account I have constructed of socially embedded reproductive preferences, and the salience of family planning and reproductive health programmes in the world, has been to show that the language of rights, never mind individual rights, is ill suited for discussions on population in a world that suffers from the Impact Inequality. Moreover, rights frequently clash, which is why unless priority rules are established, talk of rights doesn't amount to much. The material in Chapter 6, including the observations on rights, is taken from Dasgupta and Dasgupta (2017, 2024).

CHAPTER 7: PAY FOR WHAT YOU USE

The literature on common property resources is vast. Feeny et al. (1990) was an early review of empirical findings on the way (local) CPRs have long been managed. The authors pointed to local governance as the basis for cooperation in the commons. Ghate, Jodha and Mukhopadhyay (2008) is a key set of essays on the character of communitarian governance of CPRs in contemporary South Asia, from which I have borrowed material on the subject in Chapter 7. Readers will recognise that ideas of trust, reciprocity and social networks, on which that chapter is based, are closely related to the concept of 'social capital' developed by Coleman (1987) and Putnam (1993), among many others. Dasgupta (2000) demonstrates that one can analyse the basis of cooperation either by starting with the idea of social capital or by the route I have followed in Chapter 7. Conflicts over resources are stark examples of non-cooperation. Blench (2004, 2024) offers vivid accounts of conflicts between farmers and herders in present-day North-Central Nigeria. His narratives bear more than a passing resemblance to accounts of the Johnson County War between homesteaders and cattlemen in Wyoming, USA, in 1889–93, movingly portrayed in the film *Shane*. Destruction of CPRs accompanies the degradation of the corresponding ecosystems. On the plight of indigenous populations caused by multinational extractive companies, see Lema and Vasquez (2022).

CHAPTER 8: A NEW MEASURE OF WEALTH

The equivalence between inclusive wealth and wellbeing across the generations was stated and proved in Dasgupta and Mäler (2000) and extended to a wider range of economies than were included previously, in Arrow, Dasgupta and Mäler (2003b). UNU-IHDP and UNEP (2012) was the first attempt at estimating changes in inclusive wealth in a list of over 120 countries towards the end of the twentieth century. On the science and practice of sustainability analysis, see Matson, Clark and Andersson (2016) and Perrings and Kinzig (2021). Managi and Kumar (2018), a UNEP-sponsored publication, is the source of Fig. 8.1. On methods for determining the value of environmental amenities, see the excellent text by Freeman (2003). Haque, Murty and Shyamsundar (2011) is an illuminating collection of case studies determining the productive value (or use value) of ecosystems. Before consulting the case studies in the latter publication, readers should read the methodological essay by Vincent (2011) that opens the volume. The collection is particularly interesting and important because it estimates the use value of ecosystems in a poor part of the world, South Asia, and it does so by studying the productivity of ecosystems, not by asking people how much they are willing to pay for goods and services.

CHAPTER 10: THE VALUE OF
THE WORLD AROUND US

In a wide-ranging and moving essay on death and the afterlife, the philosopher Samuel Scheffler (2013) has also observed that our own lives would be diminished if there are to be no future people. Pedersen (2025) is an incisive study of the rights Nature is seen to possess in Hindu ethics.

References

Arrow, K.J., Dasgupta, P. and Mäler, K.G. (2003a), 'Evaluating Projects and Asserting Sustainable Development in Imperfect Economies', *Environmental and Resource Economics* 26(4): 647–85.

Arrow, K.J., Dasgupta, P. and Mäler, K.G. (2003b), 'The Genuine Savings Criteria and the Value of Population', *Economic Theory*, 21(2/3), 217–25.

Barbier, E.B. (1994), 'Valuing Environmental Functions: Tropical Wetlands', *Land Economics* 70(2): 155–73

Barbier, E.B. (2011), *Scarcity and Frontiers: How Economies Have Developed Through Natural Resource Exploitation* (Cambridge: Cambridge University Press)

Barrett, S. (2003), *Environment and Statecraft: The Strategy of Environmental Treaty-Making* (Oxford: Oxford University Press)

Barrett, S. (2012), 'Credible Commitments, Focal Points and Tipping: The Strategy of Climate Treaty Design', in Hahn, R. and Ulph, A. (eds), *Climate Change and Common Sense: Essays in Honour of Tom Schelling* (Oxford: Oxford University Press)

Barrett, S., Dasgupta, A., Dasgupta, P. et al. (2020), 'Social Dimensions of Fertility Behavior and Consumption Patterns in the Anthropocene', *Proceedings of the National Academy of Sciences* 117(12): 6300–7

Benhabib, J., Bisin, A. and Jackson, M.O. (eds) (2011), *Handbook of Social Economics* (Amsterdam: North Holland)

Blench R. (2004), *Natural Resources Conflicts in North-Central Nigeria* (London: Mandaras Publishing)

Blench, R. (2024), *A Trophic Cascade in Nigerian Vegetation and Its Implications for Farmer-Herder Conflict*, working paper, https://www.academia.edu/124002886

Bongaarts, J. (2011), 'Can Family Planning Programs Reduce High Desired Family Size in Sub-Saharan Africa?', *International Perspectives on Sexual and Reproductive Health* 37(4): 209–16

Bongaarts, J. (2016), 'Development: Slow Down Population Growth', *Nature* 530: 409–12

Bongaarts, J. (2019), 'Population: The Current State and Future Prospects', in Dasgupta, P., Raven, P.H. and McIvor, A. (eds), *Biological Extinction: New Perspectives* (Cambridge: Cambridge University Press), pp. 193–213

Bongaarts, J. (2020), 'Trends in Fertility and Fertility Preferences in sub-Saharan Africa: the roles of education and family planning programs', *Genus: Journal of Population Studies*, open access, https://doi.org/10.1186/s41118-020-00098z

Bowman, W.D. and Hacker, S.D (2023), *Ecology* (6th edition, Oxford: Oxford University Press)

Brundtland, G.H. (1987), *Our Common Future: Report of the World Commission on Environment and Development* (Oxford: Oxford University Press)

Carson, R. (1951), *The Sea Around Us* (Oxford: Oxford University Press)

Carson, R (1962), *Silent Spring* (New York: Houghton Mifflin)

Ceballos, G. and Ehrlich, P.R. (2023), 'Mutilation of the Tree of Life via Mass Extinction of Animal Genera', *Proceedings of the National Academy of Science* 120(39): e2306987120

Ceballos, G., Ehrlich, P.R. and Raven, P.H. (2020), 'Vertebrates on the Brink as Indicators of Biological Annihilation and the Sixth Mass

Extinction', *Proceedings of the National Academy of Science* 117(24): 13596–602

Chopra, K. and Gulati, S.C. (2001), *Migration, Common Property Resources, and Environmental Degradation* (New Delhi: Sage Publications)

Coleman, J.S. (1987), 'Norms as Social Capital', in Radnistzky, G. and Bernholtz, P. (eds), *Economic Imperialism: The Economic Approach Applied Outside the Field of Economics* (New York: Paragon House), pp. 133–55

Das, S. and Vincent, J.R. (2009), 'Mangroves Protected Villages and Reduced Death Toll During Indian Super Cyclone', *Proceedings of the National Academy of Sciences* 106(18): 7357–60

Dasgupta, P. (2000), 'Economic Progress and the Idea of Social Capital', in Dasgupta, P. and Serageldin, I. (eds), *Social Capital: A Multifaceted Perspective* (Washington, DC: World Bank)

Dasgupta, P. (2021), *The Economics of Biodiversity: The Dasgupta Review* (London: HM Treasury, online); published with additional technical material as Dasgupta (2024)

Dasgupta, P. (2024), *The Economics of Biodiversity: The Dasgupta Review* (Cambridge: Cambridge University Press)

Dasgupta, Aisha and Dasgupta, P. (2017), 'Socially Embedded Preferences, Environmental Externalities, and Reproductive Rights', *Population and Development Review* 43(3): 405–41

Dasgupta, Aisha and Dasgupta, P. (2022), 'Population Overshoot', in Arrhenius, G., Bykvist, K., Campbell, T. and Finneron-Burns, E. (eds), *The Oxford Handbook of Population Ethics* (Oxford: Oxford University Press), pp. 490–518

Dasgupta, Aisha and Dasgupta, P. (2024), 'Human Population and the Biosphere', *Population and Development Review*, forthcoming

Dasgupta, P. and Mäler, K.-G. (2000), 'Net National Product, Wealth, and Social Well-Being', *Environment and Development Economics* 5(1): 69–93

Dasgupta, P., Mitra, T. and Sorger, G. (2019), 'Harvesting the Commons', *Environmental and Resource Economics* 72(3): 613–36

Dasgupta, P., Raven, P.H. and McIvor, A. (eds) (2019), *Biological Extinction: New Perspectives* (Cambridge: Cambridge University Press)

Diamond, J. (1997), *Guns, Germs, and Steel: The Fates of Human Societies* (New York: W. W. Norton)

Douglas, M. and Isherwood, B.C. (1979), *The World of Goods* (New York: Basic Books)

Durrett, R. and Levin, S.A. (1996), 'Spatial Models of Species-Area Curves', *Journal of Theoretical Biology* 179(2): 119–27

Easterlin, R. (1974), 'Does Economic Growth Improve the Human Lot? Some empirical evidence', in David, P.A. and Reder, M. (eds), *Nations and Households in Economic Growth: Essays in Honor of Moses Abramowitz* (New York: Academic Press)

Ehrlich, P.R. and Ehrlich, A. (1981), *Extinction: The Cause and Consequences of the Disappearance of Species* (New York: Random House)

Ehrlich, P.R. and Ehrlich, A. (2008), *The Dominant Animal: Human Evolution and the Environment* (Washington, DC: Island Press)

Ehrlich, P. R., and Holdren, J.R. (1971), 'Impact of Population Growth', *Science*, 171(3977), 1212–1217.

Ehrlich, P.R., Ceballos, G. and Dirzo, R. (2024), *Before They Vanish: Saving Nature's Populations – and Ourselves* (Baltimore, MD: The Johns Hopkins University Press)

Feeny, D., Berkes, F., McCay, B. J. and Acheson, J. M. (1990), 'The Tragedy of the Commons: Twenty-two years later', *Human Ecology* 18(1): 1–19

REFERENCES

Folke, C., Carpenter, S., Walker, B. et al. (2004), 'Regime Shifts,
Resilience, and Biodiversity in Ecosystem Management', *Annual
Review of Ecology, Evolution, and Systematics* 35(1): 557–81

Frankopan, P. (2023), *The Earth Transformed: An Untold Story* (London:
Bloomsbury)

Freeman III, A. M. (2003), *The Measurement of Environmental and
Resource Values: Theory and Methods* (Washington, DC: Resources
for the Future)

Gale, D. (1986), 'Bargaining and Competition, Part I: Characterization'
and 'Bargaining and Competition, Part II: Existence', *Econometrica*
54: 785–806 and 807–18

Gardner, M. (1970), 'The Fantastic Combinations of John Conway's
New Solitaire Game of "Life"', *Scientific American* 223(4): 120–3

Ghate, R., Jodha, N.S. and Mukhopadhyay, P. (eds) (2008), *Promise,
Trust, and Evolution: Managing the Commons of South Asia* (Oxford:
Oxford University Press)

Gordon, H.S. (1954), 'The Economic Theory of a Common
Property Resource: The Fishery', *Journal of Political Economy*
62(2): 124–42

Griffin, J. (1986), *Well-being: Its Meaning, Measurement, and Moral
Importance* (Oxford: Clarendon Press)

Haque, A.K.E., Mukhopadhyay, P., Nepal, M. and Shammin, Md R.
(eds) (2022), *Climate Change and Community Resilience: Insights
from South Asia* (Singapore: Springer), open access, https://link.
springer.com/book/10.1007/978-981-16-0680-9

Haque, A.K.E, Murty, M. and Shyamsundar, P. (eds) (2011),
Environmental Valuation in South Asia (Cambridge: Cambridge
University Press)

Hardin, G. (1968), 'The Tragedy of the Commons', *Science* 162(3859):
1243–8

IPBES (2019), *Assessment Report on Biodiversity and Ecosystem Services* (Bonn: UN Campus), https://doi.org/10.5281/senodo3831673

IPCC (2023), *Climate Change 2023: Synthesis Report* (Geneva: IPCC), doi:10.59327/IPCC.AR6-97891691647.001

Jodha, N.S. (1986), 'Common Property Resources and the Rural Poor', *Economic and Political Weekly* 21: 1169–81

Jodha, N.S. (2001), *Living on the Edge: Sustaining Agriculture and Community Resources in Fragile Environments* (Delhi: Oxford University Press)

Kolbert, E. (2014), *The Sixth Extinction: An Unnatural History* (New York: Henry Holt and Co.)

Kuznets, S. (1941), *National Income and Its Composition, 1919–1938* (New York: National Bureau of Economic Research)

Landes, D. (1998), *The Wealth and Poverty of Nations: Why Some Are So Rich and Some So Poor* (London: W. W. Norton)

Laurence, W.F., Lovejoy, T.E., Vasconcelos, H.L. et al. (2002), 'Ecosystem Decay of Amazonian Forest Fragments: A 22-Year Investigation', *Conservation Biology* 16(3): 605–18

Layard, R. and De Neve, J.-E. (2023), *Wellbeing: Science and Policy* (Cambridge: Cambridge University Press)

Lema, D. and Vasquez, A. (2022), 'Forced Displacement of Indigenous Peoples in the Amazon Caused by Environmental Hardship: A Case for Human Security', *Peace Human Rights Governance* 6(2): 159–80

Levin, S.A. (ed.) (2001), *Encyclopedia of Biodiversity* (1st edition, New York: Academic Press), vols 1–5

Levin, S.A. (ed.) (2009), *The Princeton Guide to Ecology* (Princeton, NJ: Princeton University Press)

Lovejoy, T.E. and Hannah, L. (eds) (2019), *Biodiversity and Climate Changes: Transforming the Biosphere* (New Haven, CT: Yale University Press)

Lovelock, J. (1979), *The Ages of Gaia: A Biography of Our Living Earth* (Oxford: Oxford University Press)

Luce, R.D. and Raiffa, H. (1957), *Games and Decisions* (New York: John Wiley & Sons)

MacArthur, R.M. and Wilson, E.O. (1967), *Island Biogeography* (Princeton, NJ: Princeton University Press)

Maddison, A. (2001), *The World Economy: A Millennial Perspective* (Paris: OECD)

Maddison Project Database (2020), https://www.rug.nl/ggdc/historical development/maddison/releases/maddison-project-database-2020

Managi, S. and Kumar, P. (2018), *Inclusive Wealth Report 2018: Measuring Progress Towards Sustainability* (New York: Routledge)

Markandya, A. and Murty, M.N. (2004), 'Cost–Benefit Analysis of Cleaning the Ganges: Some Emerging Environment and Development Issues', *Environment and Development Economics* 9(1): 61–81

Matson, P., Clark, W.C. and Andersson, K. (2016), *Pursuing Sustainability: A Guide to the Science and Practice* (Princeton, NJ: Princeton University Press)

MEA (2005), *Ecosystems and Human Well-Being: Synthesis* (Washington, DC: Island Press)

Micklethwait, J. and Wooldridge, A. (2003), *A Future Perfect: The Challenge and Promise of Globalization* (New York: Random House)

Mora, C., Tittensor, D.P., Adl, S. et al. (2011), 'How Many Species Are There on Earth and the Oceans?', *PLoS Biology* 9(8): e1001127, open access, doi:10.1371/journal.pbio.1001127

Mukhopadhyay, P. (2008), 'Heterogeneity, Commons, and Privatization: Agrarian Institutional Change in Goa', in Ghate, R., Jodha, N.S. and Mukhopadhyay, P. (eds), *Promise, Trust and Evolution: Managing the Commons of South Asia* (Oxford: Oxford University Press)

Nagel, T. (1986), *The View from Nowhere* (Oxford: Oxford University Press)

Pedersen, K. (2025), 'The Rights of Nature and Hindu Ethics', in Sharma, A. and Penumala, P. (eds) (2025), *The Bloomsbury Handbook of Hindu Ethics* (London: Bloomsbury).

Perrings, C. and Kinzig, A. (2021), *Conservation: Economics, Science, & Policy* (Oxford: Oxford University Press)

Pigou, A.C. (1920), *The Economics of Welfare* (London: Macmillan)

Pikovsky, A., Rosenblum, M and Kurths, J. (2001), *Synchronization: A Universal Concept in Nonlinear Sciences* (Cambridge: Cambridge University Press)

Pimm, S.L. and Raven, P.H. (2019), 'The State of the World's Biodiversity', in Dasgupta, P., Raven, P.H. and McIvor, A. (eds) (2019), *Biological Extinction: New Perspectives* (Cambridge: Cambridge University Press), pp. 80–112

Prest, B.C., Wingenroth, J. and Rennert, K. (2019), *The Social Cost of Carbon Reaching a New Estimate* (Washington, DC: Resources for the Future)

Putnam, R.D., with Leonardi, R. and Nanetti, R.Y. (1993), *Making Democracy Work: Civic Traditions in Modern Italy* (Princeton, NJ: Princeton University Press)

Richardson, K., Steffen, W., Lucht, W. et al. (2023), 'Earth Beyond Six of Nine Planetary Boundaries', *Science Advances* 9(37): 1–16

Ridley, M (2010), *The Rational Optimist: How Prosperity Evolves* (New York: Harper)

Rockström, J., Steffen, W., Noone, K. et al. (2009), 'A Safe Operating Space for Humanity', *Nature* 461(7263): 472–5

Rosenzweig, M.L. (1995), *Species Diversity in Space and Time* (Cambridge: Cambridge University Press)

Schama, S. (1995), *Landscape and Memory* (London: HarperCollins)

Scheffler, S. (2013), *Death and the Afterlife* (Oxford: Oxford University Press)

Schell, J. (1982), *The Fate of the Earth* (New York: Avon)

Scholes, R.J. and Walker, B.H. (1993), *An African Savanna: Synthesis of the Nylsvley Study* (Cambridge: Cambridge University Press).

Sheldrake, M. (2020), *Entangled Life: How Fungi Make Our World, Change Our Minds, and Shape Our Futures* (London: Bodley Head)

Shyamsundar, P. (2008), 'Decentralization, Devolution, and Collective Action – A Review of International Experience 1', in Ghate, R., Jodha, N. and Mukhopadhyay, P. (eds), *Promise, Trust and Evolution: Managing the Commons of South Asia* (Oxford: Oxford University Press)

Sidgwick, H. (1907), *The Methods of Ethics* (7th edition, London: Macmillan)

Siegel, T., A. Magrach, W. Laurance, and D. Luther (2024), 'A Global Meta-Analysis of the Impacts of Forest Fragmentation on Biotic Mutualisms and Antagonisms', *Conservation Biology*, open access, https//doi.org/101111/cobi.14206.

Solow, R. M. (1957), 'Technical Change and the Aggregate Production Function', *Review of Economics and Statistics* 39(3): 312–20

Somanathan, E., Prabhakar, R. and Mehta, B.S. (2009), 'Decentralization for cost-effective conservation', *Proceedings of the National Academy of Sciences* 106(11): 4143–7

Stern, N.H. (2015), *Why Are We Waiting? The Logic, Urgency, and Promise of Tackling Climate Change* (Cambridge, MA: MIT Press)

Strogatz, S. (2003), *Sync: The Emerging Science of Spontaneous Order* (New York: Penguin)

Sullivan, J.M., Constant, V. and Lubchenco, J. (2019), 'Extinction Threats to Life in the Oceans and Opportunities for Their Amelioration', in Dasgupta, P., Raven, P.H. and McIvor, A. (eds) (2019), *Biological Extinction: New Perspectives* (Cambridge: Cambridge University Press), pp. 113–37

Temin, P. (2013), *The Roman Market Economy* (Princeton, NJ: Princeton University Press)

Thomas, D. (2019), *Fashionopolis* (London: Head of Zeus)

Tilman, D. and Downing, J.A. (1994), 'Biodiversity and Stability in Grasslands', *Nature* 367(6461): 363–7

Tilman, D., Isbell, F. and Cowles, J.M. (2014), 'Biodiversity and Ecosystem Functioning', *Annual Review of Ecology, Evolution, and Systematics* 45: 471–93

Tupy, M. and Pooley, G. (2022), *Superabundance: The Story of Population Growth, Innovation, and Human Flourishing on an Infinitely Bountiful Planet* (Washington, DC: Cato Institute)

UNEP (2022), *Inclusive Wealth Report 2022* (Nairobi: United Nations Environment Programme)

UNFPA (1995), *Programme of Action of the International Conference on Population and Development* (New York: United Nations Population Fund), Ch. 7, Sec. 3.

UNFPA (2023), *State of the World Population: 8 billion lives, Infinite Possibilities, the Case for Rights and Choices* (New York: United Nations Population Fund)

UNPD (2024), *World Population Prospects* (New York: United Nations Population Division)

UNU-IDHP and UNEP (2012), *Inclusive Wealth Report 2012: Measuring Progress Toward Sustainability* (Cambridge: Cambridge University Press)

Veblen, T. (1899), *The Theory of the Leisure Class* (New York: Macmillan)

Vincent, J. (2011), 'Valuing the Environment as a Production Input', in Haque, A.K.A., Murty, M.N. and Shyamsundar, P., eds., *Environmental Valuation in South Asia* (Cambridge: Cambridge University Press)

Wackernagel, M. and B. Beyers (2019), *Ecological Footprint: Managing Our Biocapacity Budget* (Gabriola Island, BC: New Society)

Waters, C.N., Zalasiewicz, J., Summerhayes, C. et al., (2016), 'The Anthropocene is Functionally and Stratigraphically Distinct from the Holocene', *Science* 351(6269): 1–10

Weinberg, S. (2016), *To Explain the World: The Discovery of Modern Science* (New York: Harper Perennial)

Wilson, E. O. (1992), *The Diversity of Life* (Cambridge, MA: Belknap Press of Harvard University Press)

World Bank (1992), *World Development Report* (Washington, DC: World Bank)

Index

Note: page numbers in **bold** refer to diagrams; page numbers in *italics* refer to information contained in tables. Page numbers preceded by an N refer to footnotes.

Acknowledgements

I am grateful to Albert DePetrillo of Witness Books for asking me to prepare a book for the general reader on natural capital. He and his editorial team, Jessica Anderson, Shammah Banerjee, Paul Murphy and Howard Watson have been most encouraging throughout. In preparing the text for publication, I have been much helped by Slawomir Dziarmaga, Jake Dyer, Craig Peacock and Paul Rhind-Tutt at the Faculty of Economics at Cambridge.

My education in what I now know to be ecological economics dates to 1978, when by chance I came across *EcoScience*, a treatise by Paul Ehrlich, Anne Ehrlich and John Holdren, and then in 1989, when, as a newly appointed professor at Stanford, I met Paul Ehrlich. Over the next two years, on afternoon walks in the Stanford Hills, he taught me ecology while I taught him economics. That education continued for me when, in 1991, Karl-Göran Mäler was appointed Director of the Beijer Institute of Ecological Economics, Stockholm. Because Mäler asked me to serve on the Institute's Scientific Advisory Board, and Ehrlich was a Member, Ehrlich's and my walks continued at the Institute's annual Board meeting in the island of Askö, but we were now accompanied by Kenneth Arrow, Simon Levin and Mäler. Their influence, and that of those closely associated with the institute, in particular Scott Barrett, Bert Bolin, Stephen Carpenter, Carl Folke, Jane Lubchenco, Charles Perrings, Brian Walker, Anastasios Xepapadeas and Aart de Zeeuw - has been enormous. A day long visit in June 2002 to the Missouri Botanic Gardens, St Louis, under the tutelage of its President Emeritus, Peter Raven, introduced me to the community life of plants and altered my understanding of the processes that govern ecosystems.

The chapters that follow are based on lectures on the environment and economic development that I have delivered over the past several years at the annual teaching workshop of the South Asian Network for Development and Environmental Economics (SANDEE), held at the Asian Institute of Technology, Pathum Thani, Thailand. I am deeply grateful to Priya Shyamsundar and Mani Nepal, successive Directors of SANDEE, for the many discussions I have had with them on environment and development and to the participants at the workshops, too numerous to mention individually. I owe much also to discussions and correspondence over the years with Inger Anderson, Ed Barbier, Kamal Bawa, S.J. Beard, Caroline Bledsoe, John Bongaarts, Mary Colwell, Diane Coyle, Shamik Dasgupta, Zubeida Dasgupta, Anantha Duraiappah, Roger Gifford, Enamul Haque, Yusuf Hamied, James Heckman, Pushpam Kumar, Shunsuke Managi, Emily McKenzie, Pranab Mukhopadhyay, Mani Nepal, Ant Parham, Alaknanda Patel, Kusumita Pedersen, Martin Rees, Victoria Robb, Sandy Sheard, Priya Shyamsundar, Robert Solow, Alistair Ulph, Thomas Viegas, Jeff Vincent, Bhaskar Vira, Mathis Wackernagel, Ruth Waters and Rowan Williams. But the present work has been especially influenced by Aisha Dasgupta, who assumed the lead in collaborative works that form the basis of some of the central material here.

Above all I am grateful to Carol Dasgupta, whose suggestions on what to emphasise and what is superficial have been invaluable.

Partha Dasgupta, St John's College, Cambridge